Notes from the Sofa

Raymond Briggs is an award-winning author
whose bestselling books include *The Snowman,*
Father Christmas and *Ethel & Ernest.* For the
last few years Raymond has also been
writing a regular column for *The Oldie,*
"Notes from the Sofa".

The Oldie is a humorous monthly magazine
launched in 1992 by Richard Ingrams, who for
22 years was the magazine's editor following
23 years in the same post at *Private Eye.*

Dear Reader,

The book you are holding came about in a rather different way to most others. It was funded directly by readers through a new website: **Unbound**.

Unbound is the creation of three writers. We started the company because we believed there had to be a better deal for both writers and readers. On the Unbound website, authors share the ideas for the books they want to write directly with readers. If enough of you support the book by pledging for it in advance, we produce a beautifully bound special subscribers' edition and distribute a regular edition and ebook wherever books are sold, in shops and online.

This new way of publishing is actually a very old idea (Samuel Johnson funded his dictionary this way). We're just using the internet to build each writer a network of patrons. At the back of this book, you'll find the names of all the people who made it happen.

Publishing in this way means readers are no longer just passive consumers of the books they buy, and authors are free to write the books they really want. They get a much fairer return too – half the profits their books generate, rather than a tiny percentage of the cover price.

If you're not yet a subscriber, we hope that you'll want to join our publishing revolution and have your name listed in one of our books in the future. To get you started, here is a £5 discount on your first pledge. Just visit unbound.com, make your pledge and type Sofa in the promo code box when you check out.

Thank you for your support,

Dan, Justin and John
Founders, Unbound

Notes from
the Sofa

Raymond Briggs

Unbound

First published by Unbound in 2015
This edition published in 2017

Unbound
6th Floor, Mutual House, 70 Conduit Street, London W1S 2GF
www.unbound.co.uk

Text design by Carrdesignstudio.com

Art direction by Mecob
Illustration by Raymond Briggs

Grateful Acknowledgements: *The Oldie*

A CIP record for this book
is available from the British Library

ISBN 978-1-78352-130-2 (trade hbk)
ISBN 978-1-78352-170-8 (ebook)
ISBN 978-1-78352-131-9 (limited edition)
ISBN 978-1-78352-416-7 (paperback edition)

Printed in Great Britain by Clays Ltd, St Ives Plc.

1 3 5 7 9 8 6 4 2

For Liz

&

Parkinson's UK

Contents

Foreword

by Dan Kieran, CEO of Unbound

"I HEARD YOU on the radio – apparently Unbound are giving publishers a good kick up the arse. Sounds marvellous, how can I help?"

So began my first conversation with the legendary Raymond Briggs in our old office in Soho some years ago. He had come to visit us, along with the then editor of *The Oldie* Richard Ingrams and the writer and publisher of *The Oldie* James Pembroke, to talk about the possibility of doing a book. The long and lubricated lunch has become something of a rarity in publishing these days, but we went out and had one of those, and the result is now in your hands.

I could drone on about what a privilege it has been to work with one of the most loved and talented children's illustrators and writers who has ever lived. How Raymond is both genial and yet wonderfully fierce at the same time on certain subjects, or how he is that very rare species of childhood hero you meet who turns out to be a generous and extraordinarily humble, genuine and utterly brilliant man. But I won't do any of those things because he would tell me to shut up and stop boring you all with my sentimental bollocks.

What I will say is that this is the first new book from Raymond in a decade. It is unique because, as he says himself, this is a book of thoughts, ideas and memories that he has written entirely for himself, rather than for an audience of children, for the first time in his entire career. It is funny, melancholic, wise and honest, and all of us at Unbound are thrilled to have played a small part in bringing it to you. You'll love it. He's a genius.

Introduction

by Raymond Briggs

PEOPLE ARE ALWAYS asking: However did you come to be writing for *The Oldie*?

Well, what a question. I honestly can't remember; like everything else in Old Age it is lost in the mists of time. These mists shroud anything from more than six weeks ago, let alone six years. No doubt soon it will be six days, then we'll be in serious trouble. Now don't get gloomy, Briggs. This is meant to be a light-hearted introduction to a book that is supposed to be humorous.

All I remember is that copies of *The Oldie* started arriving in the post. I enjoyed looking at them but didn't say thank you as I didn't know who had sent them. Then I heard from the illustrious NAIM ATTALLAH, asking me to come and have lunch with him. I knew his name, of course, but was not sure what he did, other than it was to do with immensely expensive shops in Bond Street – jewels, silver and gold stuff, nothing much… I was asked to go this address in Frith Street in the heart of wicked Soho – such a contrast to the innocence of dear old Wimbledon Park. The whole building was painted black outside and I was shown into a very dark room, also painted black. Naim Attallah and I were the only people in the room and I formed the impression that it was his own house. He had a small gadget on the table like a glasses case (obviously containing an APP, even in those days). Whenever he put his hand on it, a waiter would silently appear and bring in the next course or more wine. Naim said, I think, that he owned *The Oldie* and casually mentioned that it was only losing thirty or forty thousand pounds a month. Huh! Peanuts, I thought, but I didn't say it. I think I've been to the same place since then and realise now that it is a sort of club, still dark and painted black inside and out.

Naim then went on to suggest that I write for *The Oldie*! Blimey! What on earth would I write about? I had done odd bits for respectable papers like the *Observer*, the *Guardian* and the *Times Ed. Supp.*, but they were mostly book reviews, fairly routine stuff. This was much more intimidating.

Still, it was a great honour to be asked to write for a national magazine when you are over seventy years old and a decade or so past retirement age. Furthermore, to be given the freedom to write about anything you like and get paid* for it!

Ye Gods! My cup runneth over. It went all down my trousers yet again.

A new lease of life for an elderly olide! So, ta Attallah! Thank you.

Raymond Briggs

*albeit tuppence ha'penny

HOWEVER, I SOON felt less intimidated because of encouragement by the legendary Richard Ingrams. He sent many hand-written notes such as this one in response to a RANT. No! "Going great guns!"

Trousers – watch out!

RANT

YESTERDAY I heard someone on the wireless happen to mention, casually! in passing! that our beloved red London buses were owned by the *FRENCH*! I was so stunned by this that I thought I must have misunderstood, so I asked my assistant to look it up on her electric gadget.

It turns out to be much worse: it's not just the Frogs, there are FIVE foreign buggers owning *our* London buses! Has this country gone mad? Can't we Brits own our own buses for godsake? There is:

Abellio – Dutch Railways

Arriva – Deutsch Bahn (Kraut)

'London' Sovereign – Veolia Transdev (Frog)

'London' United – RATP (Frog again)

Metroline – Singapore!

Also, umpteen foreign outfits own Gatwick airport. The Frogs already own our electricity and now they even own Newhaven harbour. Local residents have been forbidden to sit on their own beach!

How far will this go? Will we wake up one day to find Big Ben is owned by the Chinese? Or a Russian oligarch owns Buckingham Palace? What price St Paul's, Westminster Abbey and the Tower of London? Are they all up for grabs?

Why did we fight the War? Something about freedom from foreign domination, wasn't it? Today if Hitler wanted to invade our country, he wouldn't need to waste money and lives on Stormtroopers, tanks and Blitzkrieg. He could just buy up the whole lot without firing a shot.

Good luck to him. Who needs it? It's not ours anyway.

PS: Then today, it came on the news that the BBC had *sold* the *Radio Times*! Mind you, it was 88 years old, so like people of that age, it's as good as dead anyway. Next it will be Broadcasting House itself, already a relic, but still of some historical interest. Most of the staff have already been shunted up to SALFORD! Poor devils.

PPS: It has just been announced that 95 per cent of the Royal Mail is to be sold off! How Royal will it be *then*? This country is not going to the dogs. It's gone.

PPPS: Yet more! The RAC is to be sold. I give up.

RAYMOND BRIGGS

November 2011 – THE OLDIE 51

The **Oldie** 22/9/11

Dear Raymond
Thanks for your excellent
RANT about the bloody
foreigners taking over. You're
saving guns!

[signature]

65 Newman Street, London, W1T 3EG Tel: 020 7436 8801 Fax: 020 7436 8804
Email: editorial@theoldie.co.uk Web: www.theoldie.co.uk

Notes
from
the Sofa

OH NO, NOT AGAIN!

WHY OH WHY?

OH HECK!

NO!
OH NO!

HOW ON EARTH....?

This could be written by ME! x

The cussedness of inanimate objects

THE CUSSEDNESS OF THE INANIMATE OBJECT (TCOIO) is the bane of Old Age. While genteelly dining, you reach out for your glass of wine, not for the first time, and your sleeve catches a dessert spoon and sends it clattering to the floor. Whereupon, of course, it bounces along and secretes itself under the electric heater. Without moving the table, two chairs and the heater, it is impossible to get it out. Why did it do it?

Why do these things happen all the time? For me, FOTF – Falling on the Floor – is the big one. Lately, I've been making a daily list of FOTFs – eleven yesterday. The Force of Gravity is an important factor in all ages of life, but in Old Age it becomes dominant.

It even dominates Waitrose's tiny, all-butter mince pies. Today, I took one out of its foil cup, raised it to my eager lips – and, of course, it snapped itself in two in mid-air, fell on my trousers, bounced off and messed itself on the floor.

Grapes are the be-all and end-all of TCOIO. But they can scarcely

3

be described as inanimate. They have a powerful internal lust for mischief. Even the holy Waitrose recognises this and presents its grapes sealed in a plastic bag with a ZIP! On top of that, we are exhorted to put this sealed bag of the bouncy little devils into another bag for reasons of Health & Safety. Free-roaming grapes underfoot can cause a human being to FOTF and possibly break a bone or two. What have grapes got against us? Waitrose's insurance takes no chances, so they cover themselves with dire warnings about the Clear & Present Danger of Grapes. Then, yesterday, I was putting a small pot of Müller Light Banana & Custard into the fridge, when it got its top off and slopped itself all over slices of Sweet & Nutty Jarlsberg cheese. Müller? German? Possibly a dangerous fifth column infiltrating… But also maybe an inspirational new dish – Banana and Nutty Cheese Custard, a rare Norwegian delicacy.

Recently, the forces of TCOIO launched a triple attack on me in a single evening. I had just picked up a cup of cooked chillies, and as I turned to put it down again, the back of my hand hit the hot frying pan on the stove. The pan must

have surreptitiously vibrated its way off its ring and onto the very edge. I gave a yelp and dropped the cup. Red chilli sauce and china fragments all over the floor.

Minutes later, I was out in the passage and, as I bent over to pick up a dead leaf, our new cordless phone thrust its way out of my shirt pocket and made a suicidal dive to the floor where it fell to bits. Two batteries rolled away and, of course, one of them cunningly rolled itself under the door into the junk room. Moving with lightning speed, I grabbed the door open just in time to see the battery hurrying along to hide itself under the old spare fridge.

Half an hour later, I went to get a cooked meal out of the eye-level kitchen fridge. As I opened the door, a long horizontal dish threw itself out and crashed onto the floor at my feet. Razor-edged fragments all over the floor again. I had carefully placed the dish on a clear, open shelf at about chest level, at least three inches in. How had it juddered forwards and jammed itself bang up against the door?

TCOIO? The Courage of Injured Operatives. WWU – Workers of the World Unite!

We shall NEVAR SURRENDAR!

GRRR-OMIT!

RECENTLY, I WAS astounded to receive a request, together with a head-swelling compliment, from one of my greatest heroes.

The hero was the Right Honourable Lord, Sir Nicholas Park CEB* of 62 West Wallaby street, known to the populace as Nick Park, the supreme creator of the immortal *Wallace & Gromit*.

One of the many sad things about old age is that your heroes, if they are still living, are younger than you, often by decades. This is particularly true of Nick Park, who is, of course, still in his teens, so it was even more flattering when his note to me said: "Raymond – always an inspiration –" Ye gods! *Me* an inspiration to *HIM!!* My cup runneth over. It went all down my trousers.

The request was a simple one: would I agree to be sent a three-dimensional fibreglass model of Gromit and to colour it in any way I like? Golly! I thought. Yes! What a fun job. And it was all in aid of five hospitals in Bristol. Little did I know what fate awaited me.

The monster Gromit thing arrived, escorted by three laughing ladies. Five feet high, four feet wide across the ears and five feet long from nose to tail, weighing over half a ton. The three ladies, me and my assistant, gradually managed to drag it out of the van then struggled to get the edges of two of its giant paws onto a little trolley.

Somehow, we staggered down the garden path to the house, only to find it wouldn't go through the door. So we trundled it round to the bigger front door, but it wouldn't go in there either. We eventually decided to try and get it into the garden shed. It did go through the door – just, provided those infernal ears were perfectly aligned and tilted at exactly the right angle. This left about 12 inches on either side of it for little me to do the work.

Then the real nightmare began. Naively, I dug out my 60-year-old art student's oil paints and started colouring the beast's vast body. After a couple of days of fruitless effort it dawned on me that the palette of a 1950s fine art artiste was useless and I would need a bucketful of house paint. So, I drove off to the hardware shop and bought four litres of the stuff at £8.98 a tin. If you are ever painting the belly and bottom of a fibreglass monstrosity, I can highly recommend Dulux Weathershield Quick Dry Exterior Satin. Great covering power; beats dear old Winsor & Newton hollow.

You should try it, Park! Stop fiddling with titchy little plasticine Gromits, about four inches long; be a man and take on a five-foot monster. Try lying on your back painting Gromit's belly, paint dripping onto your face (that's another thing, I've discovered that, unlike artist's oils, house paint is *runny*). And see how many times you bang your head on those infernal ears! Also, I always wear sandals and now my feet are splattered with Dulux Exterior Green Gloss. What will my checkout ladies in Waitrose say tomorrow? Oh, Raymond! What have you done to your feet?

Yet another blow was discovering yesterday that there are not just a select few world-famous artists like me painting Gromits, but that there are now over eighty of us muggins slaving away for the greater glory of Park. This would explain the rumour that Park has already pre-sold the Gromits to a Russian oligarch for tens of millions. Before long they will be all over Red Square and dotted about the Kremlin.

CEB: Commander of the Electricity Board. This honour was bestowed upon Park in recognition of the thousands of kilowatt hours of electricity purchased by the populace watching his funny little films.

The Elephant and the Bad Baby

YESTERDAY THREE SHINY new hardback copies of one of my earliest picture books arrived: *The Elephant and the Bad Baby* by me and Elfrida Vipont, published in 1971.

Forty-three years ago! Almost before I was born. Elfrida herself died in 1992 at 90 years of age! This was a recent edition of our book in Chinese.

It brought back memories of the day I took the finished artwork up to Hamish Hamilton, the publisher, in London.

In those prehistoric days, artwork was mounted, can you believe, on cardboard! How primitive can you get? If you suggested this to a present-day art student, they would think you had gone mad. Thirty or forty sheets of cardboard weighing approximately a quarter of a ton. Soon after this, I discovered the new-fangled holiday cases with wheels on the bottom and a telescopic handle on the top. Yoof today doesn't know it's born. They don't need wheels, telescopic handles, strength, resolve or determination; it's all done by electric. Even this bit I'm writing now has to go electric. *The Oldie* Powers That Be will not accept anything on paper. They don't know where it's been. Furthermore, not only is there no cardboard for students, there is no paper either. They all draw on plastic! Yuk!

That day in 1971, when I lugged the artwork up to London, was the very day when the new money came in. My wife, Jean, and I were in the coffee bar on the platform at Haywards Heath station. Together with the barman we were absorbed in the new coins. No half crowns! No shillings! A hundred pennies (so-called "pence") to the pound – not 240!

What a swindle! No tanners, no bobs, no threepenny bits!

The train came in and, still absorbed in it all and talking about it, we got on board. A couple of minutes later, I let out a shriek: Aagh! I've left the artwork in the coffee bar! Months and months of work – my entire earnings for a whole year.

Balcombe next stop – but when?

When? At long last, Balcombe arrived – we leapt out and ran downstairs to the ticket office. Very sorry, but could you possibly phone Haywards Heath station for me, please? I've left a valuable portfolio in the coffee bar. The jobsworth in the ticket office stared blankly at me, shook his head and pointed wordlessly to the phone box. I dived across to it, then swerved back again. Have you got the number? Once again, he shook his head without uttering a word.

Back in the box, I seized a telephone directory, but it was fastened to a metal bar which passed right through the pages. I had to swivel it up to a horizontal position so I could open it. At last! Then – no light! Dark ticket hall, pitch-black phone box.

Couldn't see a thing. Gave up. Went back to the platform. Waited several years for a train. Got to Haywards Heath, leapt out, charged down the platform to the coffee bar, burst open the door – Have you... Here you are, mate, said the smiling barman, handing me my portfolio. I thought you'd be back before long.

I felt like kissing his hand. A latter-day saint. Thank goodness I didn't – in those days I could have been arrested.

Briggs the tea-leaf

I AM A CRIMINAL. A common thief. I have three confessions to make.

ONE: Every week I get two breaded lemon soles from Waitrose. These delicate items are packed extra carefully into the correct Waitrose cool bag.

One week, they were so carefully packed I didn't find them until I opened our fridge at home. Oh dear... don't remember these at the checkout... hastily dug out receipt... no fish on it.

What do I do? Phone them? Drive five miles back? Forget it?

"That which is done cannot be undone." Not without a lot of fiddle-arse anyway. Forget it.

TWO: Last autumn I saw an advertisement for a crate of wine. It sounded good and also amazingly cheap. I thought: "I might send for that..."

A few days later, I came home to find a large cardboard box on the step. Puzzled, I dragged it indoors and opened it. Wine! That box I was going to order... did I do it? Can't remember... must have done... the aged brain.

So easy nowadays – phone up,

name, postcode, card number... all done in a couple of minutes. Of course you can forget.

A few days later, came home, *another* box on the step exactly like the first one. Address on top said Ivy Cottage, just up the lane. What a coincidence, they ordered the same wine as me! Gave them a ring, they said they would collect, which they did, though I never saw them.

A few weeks later, when my box was empty, I was dumping it by the bin. It rolled over and there on the bottom was a label: Ivy Cottage. Oh, dear. "That which is undone..."

THREE: At the Queen's birthday garden party we were all drinking champagne in the Palace and were then ushered into the garden. I was still holding a full glass, and when it was empty I looked for somewhere to put it down, but there was nowhere except the lawn itself.

Just then, we were rounded up to be presented to Her Majesty and I realised I could not shake hands with the Queen whilst holding a glass in the other hand, so I hurriedly thrust it into my jacket pocket. Later, half asleep on the train, there was something prodding into my side. I felt in my pocket and took out the glass, engraved with the Royal Coat of Arms. Oh dear.

So I have stolen from Waitrose, defrauded a wine merchant and robbed Her Majesty the Queen.

For once I don't blame the parents. I do blame the school, which was a so-called grammar school in South London called Rutlish.

A pupil there a few years before me was one George Neville Heath, who oldies will remember was a sadistic serial killer of women; hanged, of course. Then, a few years after me, came someone called John Major, a one-time Prime Minister, not hanged.

With a background like that, what hope have I?

No fridge, no freezer, no flush, no fone...

SEVENTY YEARS AGO I was evacuated to two spinster "aunties" in Dorset. As a five-year-old I looked upon them as very old ladies, but years later I realised they can only have been in their forties. They were two of the thousands of women condemned to spinsterhood by the Great War. For a child at that time, the world seemed to be full of aunties.

They lived in a small stone cottage of only three rooms, with massive walls, tiny windows and a curving stone staircase.

The week I arrived, the aunties were rejoicing that, at long last, the one and only cold tap had been moved inside the cottage. This, together with the luxury of a sink and a state-of-the-art plug hole.

Cooking was done on a gas stove fed by a cylinder that also provided two feeble gas mantles. Upstairs in the one bedroom, there was no lighting. The wireless was powered by a massive glass battery and, because of the expense, was switched on only once a day for the nine o'clock news.

The simplicity of life then seems almost unbelievable today. Just listing the things that were not there: no television, LPs, CDs or cassettes. No music at all. No central heating, fridge, freezer, washing machine, dishwasher or vacuum cleaner. No oil or electricity. No telephone.

Also, there was no bathroom, shower or flush lavatory. The only heating was the coal fire in the living room, with a blackened kettle always sitting on it.

The lavatory was an Elsan in a tin shed under the apple tree. A farm worker came and emptied it once in a while.

No one was allowed to urinate in it or it would have filled up in a day or two.

I was told to pee in the hedge, and the very ladylike aunties peed in a bucket in the kitchen.

Primitive it may have been, but at least there was no computer, e-mail or internet. Also, there were no holidays, no shop and no car. One bus a week.

Paradise Lost.

A chicken-and-egg situation

MY PRIVATE PREMISES have been colonised by a chicken. My human rights have been infringed. My life is no longer my own. I have been cast into the role of mother, domestic servant, cleaner, carer and guardian. To whom can I appeal?

The council? The police? Migration Watch? Could it be an illegal chicken, lacking a visa? Strictly speaking, it is a squatter. Is squatting illegal? If so, does the law apply to squatting chickens? Except when they are strutting about, all chickens squat most of the time, don't they? That's when they lay their eggs, isn't it? That's another

thing – no eggs. She (he? it?) has been residing here for over ten weeks now, and despite my devoted care and considerable expense, there has not been a single egg.

At first, I bought chick feed, but her ladyship turned up her beak at that and devoured the much more expensive wild bird food. The last bag was £10 and was gone in a couple of weeks. £250 a year for a useless chick!

Together with all these responsibilities there is now anxiety. Foxes. She struts about the garden all day, head in the air, as if she owns the place. She attacks all wild birds that come to steal her food, even crows. Rooks, with their huge beaks and bare faces, she does not attack. I can't say I blame her.

She almost certainly knows nothing of foxes. At any moment one could appear, and seconds later she'd be eaten. If we'd known in advance we could have eaten her ourselves, but on second thought that is unthinkable. She is now virtually a member of the family, so that would almost be cannibalism.

This whole rigmarole began one morning, while walking up the garden in pouring rain, seeing a friend to her car, we saw this small, black, bedraggled bird creeping through the grass towards us. Is it a blackbird? No, it's slightly too big; a moorhen, perhaps? But then, as it came nearer, we saw its claws, so it was not a water bird. Also, it was coming towards us, so we knew it must be domesticated. It could only be a chicken.

A day or two later, Marketa, a Czech woman who was staying with us, got a fright. She was in the coal shed and suddenly saw this large, black bird, on top of the coal, flapping its wings in the darkness. "Can't you put it in the garden shed?" she wailed.

I put a heap of straw on top of the coal to make the chicken more comfortable, but in the end I did move her to the garden shed.

Where had she come from? I made diligent enquiries of all the neighbours, the village shop and the pub, but no one knew of a missing chicken.

She now appears to be fully grown. The glossy black feathers are a beautiful, very dark green, and each feather has a curving white edge and a golden plume along its spine.

All very lovely, but the mess she makes in the shed! Poos all over the floor, the shelf, and the old-fashioned pram. She likes perching on its hood. Straw everywhere. She is very bossy. If she sees an open door, she has to go through it. I've found her in the passage, the bathroom and the kitchen, together with yet more poos. What is to be done?

It's a chicken-poo-and-no-egg situation.

P.S. But! This very day, for the first time, I saw her squatting inside the pram, under the hood. Oh, heck! Yet another place to clean. But when I went over to inspect the mess, there, on the baby's pillow were TWO EGGS!

Ye Gods! All is forgiven, Chicky.

STUFF

BY the time you are 70, you have been acquiring STUFF for over half a century. Books, guides, maps, LPs, video tapes, sound tapes and CDs. We even have some pre-historic 78s for Heaven's sake. Oh… and 35 mm slides – boxes and boxes of them. Come to think of it, that means there must be a projector buried somewhere…

Now there are DVDs showering out of every newspaper. We have over 20 already and have not played one of them. Never seem to have the time.

There are radio programmes recorded 20, 30 years ago. "Oh look! Jazz Record Requests 1976. I think I'll play it now." It never happens. They are never played.

There is a shelf ten feet long, crammed with LPs. Heaven knows how many. All now technically obsolete, but still playable. Do we ever play them? Does anyone? Why do we keep them?

If you support a worthy organisation – the National Trust, National Art Collections Fund, the RA – they will keep sending you socking great magazines with umpteen leaflets inside. The latest RA pack weighed 1 lb 2 ozs, the National Art Collections Fund 1 lb 6 ozs, but the outright champion was the National Trust, weighing in at a stately 1 lb 12 ozs. Will we ever have time to read even a fraction of this STUFF? Whilst listening to a 40-year-old LP perhaps? They usually lie around in their plastic wrappers 'til the next issue thuds through the letterbox.

This isn't a home, it's a warehouse. Every week a box of STUFF goes off to the charity shop, so we can still have room to shuffle about between the stacks, but we can never get it clear.

These "minimalist" interiors seen on the television and in flash magazines – where on earth is all their STUFF? It's got to be somewhere. After all, it's the stuff of life. Don't these people have a life? Where are the cats, the dogs, the children and all their STUFF?

Despite all our efforts, it still piles up, and now we're over 70 the time left to deal with it is running out fast.

Our executor is going to have a helluva job.

P.S. Sorry, I forgot to mention the garage. We used to keep the cat in it.

Diving in

LATELY, I HAVE been making a list of my major faux pas from the last few years. The older you get, the longer the list becomes: the faltering brain...

Where was I? Oh yes, number one: Liz and I had been to see the David Hockney film, *A Bigger Splash* in Brighton. When we came out, we wandered round looking for somewhere to eat and came across an ordinary-looking place in Hove. Inside, it turned out to be quite posh. Having ordered, we started talking about the film and

I said: "It was good that bit when they were in New York and Mo says to Hockney: 'It's a pity Celia couldn' coom. Did she laak it when she caame before?'" I was putting on a Yorkshire accent, which I think I'm quite good at, having been incarcerated in Catterick Camp for two years in the fifties. "'Noo,'" said Hockney. "She thowt it were orl a bit moockay and the people were orl a bit froompay.'"

New York described as "mucky" and the people as "frumpy" was brilliant, I thought. But Liz was not listening to my wonderful mimicry; she was gazing straight past me, looking dazed. "What's the matter?'"I said.

She replied in a stunned whisper: "He heard what you said."

'What are you talking about?'

She leaned forward to whisper: "He's sitting just behind you!"

'Who, for heaven's sake?' I said. "Who is sitting just behind me?"

She leaned even further forward, making nervous little pointing movements with her hand at table level, and hissed at me: "David Hockney is sitting just behind you!"

"Oh, for God's sake," I said, turning round, "don't be so bloody stup – oh oh oh, my God..."

There he was, the man himself, almost close enough to shake hands. We had just seen Hockney in Paris, London, New York and LA, and now here he was in Hove!

I didn't know whether to write an apologetic note saying I was an admirer and pass it to the waiter, or go down to the Gents in the basement and hang myself.

In the end, I did neither. I just buried my face in the wine list, then ordered another bottle and a large brandy.

There were some other faux pas... but I can't remember now...

Cycling salvation

WHY HAS THE world gone cycling mad? It's on its way to becoming the new football. Heaven help us!

But for me, cycling was once my salvation. My mum had sent me to Sunday School, as it was the respectable, middle-class thing to do, though my parents never went to church themselves and were not middle class. Sunday School turned out to be even worse than church. We sat round in a circle of hard, wooden chairs in the gloomy church hall. Here an old

lady told us about this foreign chap with long hair and a beard, who wore something like my dad's old dressing gown and got himself killed hundreds of years ago, out in the desert somewhere. And it was all about our sins! Sins? Golly! It certainly didn't apply to me, I hadn't done any sins yet; I was looking forward to getting started, but as I was only eleven, the sins would have to wait for a bit.

Then somehow I discovered the CTC, the Cyclists' Touring Club. The sinful Cyclists' Touring Club luring wicked children away from Sunday School. It was perfect, we set out at ten o'clock on Sunday mornings, exactly the same time as soppy Sunday School. Hooray! The ideal escape. Even Mum couldn't object to this healthy outdoor activity – fresh air and exercise in the company of responsible adults in long tweedy skirts or plus fours.

We would meet the others at Mitcham Green, then 20 or more of us would cycle out into the Surrey hills. This was long before the Russian oligarchs had colonised most of the leafy arbours there.

Certainly cyclists in those days looked very different to the helmeted, neon-clad spacemen we see flashing along our country lanes today. With their plus fours, the men wore light cotton jackets in pale creamy colours. Cycling shoes had long, fold-over tongues that lay on top of the shoe itself. A few members of the group had "toe clips". Really wild. No one wore a hat of any sort, let alone a helmet, but most of us had drop handlebars. Very sporty. These were designed to make your body more streamlined when tearing along at breathtaking speed. Behind the saddle was always the black leather saddle bag, and neatly rolled on top of it was the

yellow oilskin cape; inside this was the yellow oilskin "sou'wester", as worn by North Atlantic lifeboat crews.

Everyone had mudguards and a mud flap at the bottom of the front mudguard. Why on earth not? They weigh nothing, yet no cyclist today would be seen dead with mudguards, let alone a wide black mud flap as well. Now I often see cyclists, when they are overtaking my car, with a spume of mud up the middle of their backs, on their nice white T-shirts.

There were always tandems, too, rarely seen today. Husband and wife, with, of course, the husband on the front, in charge, the wife on the back, pretending to pedal but usually gazing down at her baby child in the sidecar. If I had been a mum then I doubt if I would have risked my child in one of those frail and rickety little sidecars.

Also, I used to go to Herne Hill track to watch cycle racing. There you could see the famous Reg Harris, the British sprint champion – he of the square thighs. Honestly, his thighs were as wide as they were long, unlike mine which even today are still slim and elegant.

But my most vivid cycling memory is going out into

Surrey with my dad looking for blackberries. We found a wonderful place, under the power lines suspended from huge pylons. There were masses of blackberry bushes but no ripe fruit. While we were still searching, the air became full of a tremendous hum and a deeper, throbbing rumble which seemed to fill the sky. The very ground was vibrating under our feet. As a ten-year-old I felt quite frightened. What was happening? Then we saw the endless columns of tanks, guns and lorry-loads of soldiers go thundering by.

It was just before the 6th of June 1944. Too early for blackberries.

Privilege

CAN A SUBURBAN, working-class bloke be "privileged"? Until I went into the Army, I would have said: no, of course not.

The first morning, all of us with School Certs (O-levels) were paraded, still in civvy clothes, in front of a high-ranking officer. "You men..." he said, with a significant pause, "are the cream of the intake."

Blimey, I thought, looking round at the tired and bored conscripts like myself: if we're the so-called cream, what on earth are the others like? I soon found out.

Of the thirty men in my barrack room, only three of us had the School Certificate. No one had A-levels. Only two of us had had tertiary education. No one had been to university. Four men were illiterate. We were all ordered to write postcards to our parents there and then, and these poor chaps couldn't do it. The corporal wrote the cards for them and they were just about able to scrawl their names below.

Also, we had been instructed that we need not bring anything with us except shaving kit. Some men had taken this literally and had brought just that: a shaving brush, soap and razor in a small brown paper bag stuffed into their jacket pocket. This was their entire luggage.

I had come from a working-class family but, nevertheless my mum and I had packed a suitcase full of vests, pants, socks, beautifully ironed handkerchiefs, a complete washing kit and towel, packets of biscuits, apples and a homemade fruit cake. My girlfriend had given me three packets of dried bananas and an OUP hardback copy of George Eliot's *Middlemarch*. I had packed the usual sketchbook, notebook, address book, diary, writing paper, envelopes, stamps, pens, pencils, penknife and books – all the life support essentials I thought no one ever left home without.

I realised then that some of these men came from very primitive backgrounds, the like of which I had never seen.

Thank God for Wimbledon Park. One weekend I was invited to an Army friend's home in Birmingham.

It wasn't by any means a slum, but when I discovered I had lost my pen and asked to borrow one, it turned out that amongst the family of five, there was not one pen. Nor was there a single book in the house.

Touched by history

THERE SEEMS TO be an odd difference between time in our own life and time outside it.

Last summer I found myself in Gower Street and thought I would walk along and have a look at the Slade School as I had not been back since I left in 1957. The two bench seats were still there, one on either side of the front door, so I sat down and thought: it's over fifty years since I last sat here, yet it doesn't seem all that long ago... only half a century!

If I had been sitting there in 1955 and a silver-haired, frail old chap had come tottering up with his stick and sat down beside me, we might have started chatting and he might have said: 'Do you know, young man, I was a student here myself, in about 1905.'

1905! That's ancient history! My father was five years old. It's not just before the War, it's before the First World War! If this chap was a student in 1905, he was born in about 1885 and so too old to fight in the First. Yes, they were great days... Duncan Grant, Paul Nash, both Augustus John and the wonderful Gwen John – much better than her brother, even Augustus himself said so – Ben Nicholson, and my hero, Stanley Spencer, England's greatest painter since Turner. Almost all these people have paintings in the Tate now.

"Have you got anything in the Tate yet, young man?"

"Afraid not, sir. Maybe one day..."

"Neither have I. Too late now."

I would have felt touched by history: all these legendary people having been known to this man I was talking to, and now he was talking to me.

If a present-day student had come up and started chatting, he might have been equally amazed that I had left fifty years ago, before his father was born. The sixties seem like yesterday to me, but this student's father would have been in the womb at the time, listening to the Beatles, whereas I would have been already a staid married man with a mortgage and a lawnmower; far too mature for Beatlemania. If I then went on to say I had been given deferment from National Service until 1953 and so narrowly missed the Korean War, where National Servicemen were being killed, he would have said: "Korean War? What's that? Never heard of it."

Criminal brains!

ALL KIDS GO scrumping. Well, all *boys* do, or did in the olden days. There was an alleyway beside the NFS fire station with a laden apple tree hanging over it. Very easy, even for ten-year-olds, to reach up and grab. Quite harmless, traditional childhood naughtiness – but, nevertheless, it was theft.

A slightly deeper level of theft came when John Collie, one of our chums, led us to an alleyway at the top of Alverstone Avenue. We gave him a bunk-up and he reached over the fence and grabbed

a bunch of beautiful black grapes. Unfortunately, this was just opposite the kitchen door. It burst open and a woman stormed out with a face like thunder, screaming at us. Collie dropped down and we all ran round the corner and up another alleyway where we devoured the grapes. A great treat in wartime. Theft again – but slightly more serious.

A solitary crime of my own was never completed. One evening, I was turning into our road when the street lamps came on. I looked up at the bulb and thought I'd chuck a stone at it. (Heaven knows why.) I picked up a large, flinty stone and drew back my arm – and at that very moment a bobby came round the corner. He gave me a straight look. No one else was around, and I froze in mid-throw. Then I wiggled my arm up and down, stamped about as if exercising, and ran off.

Why do kids do these things? Just devilment, I suppose. But it was odd doing it whilst alone. No wonder I became life-long self-employed.

There was another glass-smashing criminal prank when we were walking home from the Common and had wandered into a wood beside the road. We found ourselves in the spacious grounds of a huge house. It was obviously unoccupied and looked as if it had been empty for some time.

There were very large windows at the top of a wide flight of steps and suddenly one of us – not me – threw a stone at the windows. There came an enormous crash and clattering as glass fell onto the balcony. Quite exciting. So we all started doing it, hurling stone after stone amidst the cacophony of shattering glass. Eventually, we got bored and wandered off,

back to the road. There we came across a group of a dozen or more people gathered together listening to the racket and talking about it. We joined this group and listened dutifully. "All gone quiet now," one of them said. We wandered off casually, trying not to run, but bursting with laughter.

Our next country mansion crime came when we found what may have been Wimbledon Park House, also deserted. Under a tree in the garden were two magnificent ancient Rolls-Royces, open-topped, with huge headlamps and bonnets about three yards long. We climbed up a tree very close to the house and got onto the roof where we soon found a way in. Down in the basement was a room lined with glass-fronted wooden cabinets, each one containing a single bird's egg. I also found a large, hard ball, about the size of a football, and we kicked it through the streets all the way home. I then discovered it was a coconut, with a tiny point at one end and a hole at the top. For years I used it as a money box for saving sixpences. It was hard as iron.

Much luckier was my friend, Pfeff, who found an elaborate invitation to the Lord Mayor of London's Banquet, addressed to

Count Crosskeyswiascmski (that's was it sounded like anyway).

As we were leaving, a fierce old lady dressed in black (possibly a housekeeper to the Count, who was probably long gone) suddenly came charging towards us, brandishing as stick above her head. "Criminal brains!" she shrieked in a ferocious accent. "Criminal brains!" We fled, feeling quite scared.

Yet another break-in came when we found the golf club by the lake. It was boarded up, not because of being bombed, but because it was out of use and needed to be protected against vandals like us.

We soon got in and found some long, black metal cases in the billiard room. They were padlocked, but we took them as they were and busted off the padlocks in an alleyway. Then, out slid these beautiful cues with inlaid handles of ebony and ivory. We charged around on a bombsite, using them as pretend spears.

Then a bloke in shirtsleeves and braces came out of his back gate and stood smoking, watching us. He beckoned to us and we went over like lambs, "Where did you get those cues?" he asked. Someone said: "We found them up in the woods." "I'm a police officer," he said. "Wait here." He then went indoors, probably to use the phone. Again, we obeyed and just stood there. (Unthinkable today. Why didn't we just bunk off?)

Soon a Black Maria driven by a uniformed sergeant together with two plain-clothes officers arrived. They took us up to the wood near the golf club, and questioning us separately, soon found our stories didn't match. We were lying.

I'll never forget the long pause when they both stood there, silently smoking... At last one said: "Shall we run 'em in?" Another long pause... "Nah," said the other, "Let's leave it." They drove us home in the Black Maria and a plain-clothes cop led me to the front door, his hand on my shoulder. When she opened the door, my poor mum nearly died.

Digitalis

OLD AGE IS another country; we do things differently here. Or is it that Yoof does things differently *there*? Sometimes I feel I am living in a foreign country – another world. Even the dear old *Radio Times*, for decades our cosy fireside companion, offers this advice in answer to some simpleton.

"It's most likely a problem with Flash. Go to the Adobe website and make sure you've got the latest version: get adobe.com/flashplayer. If you're still having difficulty, make sure you've got cookies enabled

and perhaps update your browser, particularly if you're using Mozilla Firefox. You need version 4."

"Cookies?"' Let alone "Cookies enabled"? "Browser"? "Mozilla Firefox"? In the same piece they mention "Samsung Blu-ray" and "What about an Android app?" What, indeed. It's good to know "– it runs on all Android phones and tablet" – "Tablets"? I've got *packets* of those – Blood pressure... cholesterol... pain... "Tablets running software versions 1.6 and above, but not Honeycomb

28

tablets". What a shame. Those Honeycomb tablets sound rather nice. It features "a news ticker" and "video available to non-Flash enabled devices". So that's a relief, but I must find out if my device is non-Flash enabled or not. Where is my device anyway? I'm sure I've seen it somewhere…

It says we're "all waiting for Panasonic to fix the problem with a firmware upgrade". Such a relief again. I was about to call Mr Holmes, our village electrician, but nowadays he's getting a bit too old to come out; rickety knees or something. I must ask him about my non-Flash enabled device, he's just the man, and of course, get an update on the firmware upgrade. Not sure I've ever seen a firmware. Quite looking forward to it.

This edition gives us the long-awaited news that we can now get "buttons" so that we can share "a link on Delicious, Digg, Reddit and StumbleUpon. This replaces the old Recommend Function." That is really good news – for some time now I've been worried about my Recommend Function. StumbleUpon sounds good, too, having in the last half hour fallen over while walking the dog. There is further invaluable advice.

"Check you can receive a DVB-S2 signal." (I must do that now, excuse me.) "If you can, use these tuning parameters… Satellite: Astra 2D tp.50; Frequency: 10,847 MHz (vertical polarity)." I must check our aerial – it *was* on a vertical pole but it blew over about a month ago. "Modulation: DVB-S2 QPSK; Symbol Rate: 23.0; FEC: 8/9."

The tiresome cliché "catch up" is used ten times in these two columns. Perhaps they are trying to drop a hint to us oldies. But before I "catch up" I must go and have a lie-down.

My brain aches.

P.S. I phoned my grandson (just 13) and read him this tripe. He understood it perfectly. To him it was ABC; to me it was hieroglyphics from a distant country. But then, he is a stupid boy.

Bellows humour

"SEVENTY-SEVEN NEXT WEEK!" said Liz, beaming triumphantly across the room at me.

"What? Fahrenheit?" I said, "surely not?" "No!" she cried. "Your AGE!"

"Oh, that," I said. "Yeah... well..."

Her smugness stems from her birthday, long ago in the thirties, happening to fall soon after mine. What's a few years after all these decades?

We always like to think we're not getting any older – just a little of course, but nothing serious. We are still OK and functioning fairly well. Slightly slower, bit more tired in the evenings, but that's natural. It's just maturity. Night life? Clubs? Late night parties? Driving home after midnight in winter? Forget it. Grown out of all that juvenilia long ago.

Admittedly, the numbers are undeniable. Seventy-seven; worse still, entering the seventy-eighth year. The following birthday, (if still alive), entering the last year of the seventies. Eighty heaves into view: stand to! Moby Eighty Dick on the starboard bow! All hands on deck! Skull and Crossbones on the horizon...

Can't argue with the numbers, but then loads of people are living to be a hundred. Almost a quarter of a century to go yet. Hey ho! On we go.

But then, something comes up and hits you in the face, shattering your delusions.

Recently, I sat down with the grandchildren who were watching television. "What's up with the sound?" I said. "Nothing," they said.

But it's not on.

"Yes, it is, dumbo!" they said in chorus. Straining forward, I could just about hear the faintest whisper, a kind of wordless hiss.

Deaf? Me? Surely not. Since then I've been glancing at ads for hearing aids, not that I need one, just to be sociable – for the sake of others really...

Then, yesterday at my birthday tea, they brought in a huge cake with what looked like seventy-seven candles on it, all flaming away. After the raucous Happy Birthday song, I leaned forward to blow the candles out. I blew three enormous puffs, then gave up, almost exhausted. One or two candles went out, half a dozen flickered, but the rest stayed alight.

"Aha! I see," I said. "Very funny. They're the trick sort that don't go out."

Then the twelve-year-old leaned forward on his side of the table, gave one long steady breath and extinguished every single candle.

Amidst the smoke, they all cheered. All except me, that is.

Failing lungs? Me? Weakness? Old Age? Surely not. Not yet.

I know you can get hearing aids, just wondering now if you can get lung aids. Not that I need one. It's just a thought, in case I need to help others.

CONSIDERING

SLOW? No. We Oldies are not slow, thank you very much.

We are Considering. When Liz and I drive into a car park, we switch off the engine, apply the handbrake, then Consider Getting Out Of The Car.

What's the weather like? Looks a bit grey. Shall we take the raincoats? Will I need gloves? The forecast said cold winds. I'll just take the umbrella, shall I? Leave the coats?

Glasses! Where are my glasses? I'll need glasses in the bank. I'll go to the bank. Your glasses are in your bag. Where's my bag? In the back where you always put it.

Did you bring the prescription? No, it's in your bag. You put it there.

Just then, a cheap, flashy car skids to a halt beside us. Instantly, two juvenile delinquents spring out and stroll off, arms round one another, laughing. The girl's hair blowing in the wind.

They have no bags, no coats. They'll catch their deaths. They stroll away, still laughing.

You go to the building society. I'll go to the chemist first, more important – your pills.

Let's take the coats and the umbrella. Be on the safe side.

Then, we Get Out Of The Car.

Don't forget to lock it. Did you leave a window open for the dog? With Jess in there, don't forget to switch off the alarm.

When, eventually, we arrive at our usual café, the juvenile delinquents are already leaving it, having had their cappuccinos, espresso lattes and other pseudo-sophisticated continental crap.

Liz and I go in, take our seats at our regular table, Sophie brings our usual pot of tea and toasted currant buns with butter. We nod and smile discreetly at other oldie regulars who are quietly considering their menus.

These juvenile delinquents... whatever will become of them?

Breaking and entering

HAVING CONFESSED BEFORE about my criminal past – stealing breadcrumbed lemon soles from Waitrose and an engraved glass from Buckingham Palace – I quite forgot to mention my involvement in car crime.

I struck first in Eastbourne, a most respectable town, and in Grove Road, a most respectable street. We had driven there for an eye test and had parked in Grove Road near the optician's. After the eye test, we walked along to Camilla's Bookshop in the same street.

As we passed my car, I remembered something I wanted to get out of it, but when I tried to unlock the driver's door, the key did not work. This was in the days before remote-controlled keys. Damn! I said. I've been having difficulty unlocking the boot and now the driver's door doesn't unlock! I can put up with a faulty boot lock, but if I can't get into the car at all, it's a slightly different matter. We can't get home! Can't get the RAC card either. It's locked inside the car!

Then I noticed that the off-side rear passenger window was open at the top. About three inches. Thank God! I thought. I reached inside, but couldn't get in – too small a gap. So I took my jacket off, rolled up my shirt sleeve and thrust my skinny, bare arm inside. Then, with much grunting and groaning, I just managed to touch the door handle with my finger tips.

At last the door swung open. Thank God! We're in! Got inside, sat down, went to reach across to the glove box – funny... those green files propped between the seats...? Don't remember Liz bringing those... still, never mind. Then, as I got a hand on the glove box, I saw a tape player under the dashboard! Aaagh! My car has not got a tape player! IT'S NOT MY CAR! Help! Get me out of here! Quick! Quick! The police are on their way! I flung open the door and jackknifed myself onto the respectable Grove Road pavement, looking wildly around for the approaching irate owner, and getting ready to protest my innocence. Fortunately, no owner was in sight, I slammed the door shut and marched away to my identical blue Honda Quintet about five cars further along.

We dived into Camilla's Bookshop, a haven of peace after the crime-ridden streets of Eastbourne. Camilla kindly made us coffees and we immersed ourselves in the civilised peace of dusty second-hand books.

Cars? Who needs them?

The love of a chicken

I HAD NO idea it was possible for a human being to get fond of a chicken. Nor did I ever dream that the human being could be me. ME! Fond of a CHICKEN? Even more unbelievable was the idea that a chicken could become fond of a human being – ME again! But it has happened. She came wandering in one day, took over our garden and strutted about as if she was the owner. Now she is invading me, taking me over, as if she owns me. We're not even engaged, let alone married, but she

is potty about me. She follows me everywhere. When I open the back door, she always tries to get into the house. I wouldn't mind her being in the house at all, were it not for the poos.

She is not searching for food; she gets plenty of that at regular human being times – breakfast, lunch and evening. When I sit in the garden in the sun, with a glass of wine, she is pecking round my feet, then she often flies up and settles on my lap. If I sit out there for breakfast, she will flutter up and peck into my bowl, mostly fruit, yoghurt and All-Bran. Maybe she needs the All-Bran. I certainly do.

Yesterday she flew up and landed on my shoulders where she walked about behind my head, pecking away, not on my neck, thank goodness, but no doubt feasting on the bugs and nits which had fallen from my sparse, white hair.

She always follows me up to the car at the end of the garden and obviously would like to get in with me. Where does she want to go? I wonder. Then, when I am in the seat and before I have closed the door, I have to push her gently away with my foot. But today I must have been too old and slow, as is usual these days, and before I could get the door shut, she was inside and on my lap, pecking at the steering wheel. Look out, twerp! I cried. You'll switch the lights on and flatten the battery! After I have got her away and closed the door, she still hovers around, so once the car is moving, I'm always worried about running over her as she is so close I cannot see her.

When I arrive back, she comes scrabbling up the garden to meet me, then follows me down to the house. The shed door (her shed now) is propped half open all day, so she is free to go in and out.

In the evening at dusk, she settles down on her poo-encrusted shelf with its pile of poo-encrusted *Oldie* magazines as a mattress. When it is dark, I go out to shut her door to keep the foxes out. I then go inside and settle her down, stroking her back of smooth, chilly feathers.

There she stays all night in the darkness of the empty shed. No bedding, no light, no warmth, no one to be with, alone in the cold and silence until dawn.

I cannot help but admire her.

What
on
earth?

Who
on
earth?

Cranky, cantankerous and crotchety

THIS BIT OF mystifying rubbish fell out of an old file the other day – *old* file? 1989? That was yesterday, wasn't it? What's a mere 24 years? Peanuts. Just a quarter of a century, bat of an eyelid (slightly swollen nowadays, of course).

pettish, peevish, ill-humoured, touchy, testy, thin-skinned, waspish, petulant, cross, irascible, choleric, ill-tempered, splenetic, crabby, crabbed, cranky, grouchy, grumpy, cantankerous, crotchety, crusty, irritable, out of sorts, snappish, snappy, huffish, huffy, curt,

short, impatient, piqued, in pique, in a fume, in a pucker, in a stew

moody, sulky, dour, gloomy, dyspeptic, sullen, morose, grumpy, moping, mopish, mopey, injured, wounded, sore, offended, indignant, angry, in high dudgeon, worked up

captious, quarrelsome, fractious, complaining, querulous, cavilling, carping, antagonistic, inimical, ill-willed, hostile, argumentative, short-tempered, quarrelsome, disputatious, contrary, perverse, unaccommodating,

unkindly, unamiable, unfriendly, sour,
caustic, tart, churlish, surly, spiteful

Briggs – 11 January 1989

What on earth was it? Who dunnit? All in lower case and hand-written on what was obviously a page from a Filofax. Filofax? Remember those, fellow oldies? What happened to yours? How do we now live without them? Nearly an inch thick, packed with diary, addresses, phone numbers, notes, calendars, dates, lists and maps. All this we now have on our smart phones, iPads, ePods, rSoles, Apps and Kindlings, and all available at the touch of a button, if you can remember which buggering button to touch.

It made me dig out my own ancient Filofax, bound in dark green leather, polished as if by a craftsman, but really polished by sheer use, in and out of pockets 50 times a day. Pockets? Yes, pockets in jackets (when did I last wear one of those?); top left pocket for pens and pencils, inside pocket for wallet, lower right pocket for handkerchief, lower left pocket for Filofax – weighing about one and a half pounds. My left shoulder still droops slightly, even now. Do they still sell them, or has the firm gone bust? Swept away on the floodtide of advancing technology?

Someone said the other day that their three-and-a-half-year-old daughter had asked for an iPad. Why doesn't she ask for a book of nursery rhymes or fairy tales? It might be a help to some poor old pensioner's royalties. Does she know what a book is? She might come across one in a children's public library, if it's not been closed, and if she can find one or two book shelves amid all the desks with screens and bleeping electronic "devices".

Oh dear, this is beginning to sound a bit pettish, peevish and ill-humoured, even touchy and testy, not like me at all, but more like the person in the list at the beginning... 11 January 1989? Only seven days before my birthday. So could it have been sent as a joke birthday present? If so, it was rather caustic, tart, churlish, surly and spiteful, don't you think?

Money talks

"SO, WHAT WAS it like then, the old money?" said the youngster.

"Well, Tom, it was so much more interesting. We didn't just have pounds and pence, we had pounds, shillings and pence. Twelve pence was one shilling, 20 shillings was one pound. So two hundred and forty pence to the pound. Then of course, there was the half penny, pronounced 'ha'penny' – I do regret the loss of language – four hundred and eighty ha'pennies to the pound. Then there were the farthings,

known as 'Jennies' or 'Jennie Wrens', because they had a wren on the reverse side. Nine hundred and sixty to the pound. They were still used in my day, helping my dad on his milk round. The customer's bill might be 'Three 'n' six three, please Madam.' Three shillings and six pence three farthings, see.

"Next above the penny – that word has gone too – imbeciles today talk about 'one pence' – came the threepenny bit, which was neither copper nor silver, and was hexagonal and brass-coloured. Occasionally there were old silver threepenny bits, but these were already antique and were saved to put in Christmas puddings.

"Next in value was the sixpence, called a 'tanner' – language gone again. A tanner was, of course, half a shilling which was called a 'bob'. Then came the two-shilling piece, officially called a florin though no one ever used the word. Then came the half crown. This was worth two shillings and sixpence, or thirty pence, or one eighth of a pound, colloquially known as half a dollar because, at the time, there were four dollars to the pound. So five bob was a dollar, and two and six was half a dollar. Then came the ten bob note, half a quid, and last of all the pound note. A note, not a poxy coin of today looking like a cross between a bob and a threepenny bit and worth about tuppence ha'penny."

Just then, the youngster's children came into the room: girl sixteen, girl fourteen, boy twelve. The youngster said: "Children, Briggs has been telling me about the old money."

"Yes," I said brightly. "Look, you see it was terrific – there were two hundred and forty pennies to the pound, ten bob notes which were half a quid, half crowns, two bob bits, bobs, tanners, threepenny bits, pennies, ha'pennies and farthings…"

The younger girl gave a little scream and ran out of the room, followed by her sister saying: "Some other time, Raymond? Homework, like." The boy pretended to stifle a huge, theatrical yawn and went over to his new electric toy which he calls a "laptop".

These modern kids! How will they ever learn about life in our world today? I didn't even get on to guineas.

Telephonitis

TODAY, THE WORLD is awash with telephones. Every single person in a house has their own mobile and there are two or three cordless phones as well.

Once again, life in another age: when I left art school in 1957 and set up as a freelance commercial artist, we had no phone in my parents' house. This was an impossible situation if you were supposed to be in business. I used to rush out to the nearest public call box at the top of the road, find it occupied, then rush down to the next one on

the corner, only to find it occupied, then go back to the first one. And of course, the client could only contact me by letter, asking me to phone him. Then, at long last, just before I left home in 1958, my parents managed to get a phone, but in those days it was not at all easy.

When eventually the phone arrived, my mother was so in awe of it that for a few weeks she was too nervous to answer it, let alone make a call herself.

A further joy was the "party line". This was where you shared

41

your number with a neighbour. Then, every time you picked up your phone you would find it "engaged". Engaged by the jabber-bag across the road. Just imagine a teenage girlie today finding her phone engaged by one of her chums! Hell hath no fury like a girlie phoneless!

Even in 1963, when I got my own house on a new housing estate, you had to plead to be allowed to have a phone.

I remember almost losing my temper with the telephone official I was talking to from a call box. He was doubtful of my being qualified to have such a thing. I said I was a self-employed artist and designer and needed to be in daily touch with publishers and agencies in London. "Well, maybe," he said, but you wouldn't say your work helps the export trade, would you? "Yes," I said. "My books sell in thousands in America (lie) and so earn dollars for this country." "Oh," he said. "I see... well, I'll see what I can do..."

Unbelievable. I was offering to buy the product he was selling and pay for its services! There wasn't a war on, was there? Phones weren't rationed, were they? Yes, they were. But why? Eventually, we did get one after waiting another five weeks.

In the midst of all this, I heard the BBC correspondent, recently arrived in a flat in New York, talking about getting a phone over there. He called the phone company and they said: "Certainly, sir, how many do you want? What colours?" He was astounded. How many! What colours! At that time, in the UK all phones were black and you were lucky to be allowed *one*. Then, when he asked how soon could they be put in, the man said: "Hmm... sorry sir, can't fix it this morning, is 2.15 this afternoon OK?" *(Total collapse of BBC party.)*

All this made me believe in private enterprise. I nearly became a Tory overnight.

A severe blow

YESTERDAY I RECEIVED a "severe blow" (quoting Hoffnung) not "to my shins", but to my self-esteem. I was at Argos and had just paid for a Philips electric cutter for nose and ear hair, one of the many curses of male Old Age, so I moved from the cash counter to the waiting area. There were only four chairs and they were all occupied, so I walked past them to look at the display on the wall. Just then, a very elderly lady stood up and offered me her seat. She was obviously over 70, white haired,

not frail, but very thin and bony.

"Why are you offering me your seat?" I asked. "Well, you were moving so slowly, I thought you needed to sit down." "I was moving slowly," I said, "because I'm not going anywhere – just over to look at the wall, about five yards."

We did not come to blows, of course, as I was more astounded than indignant. It was odd enough a woman giving up her seat to a man, but a really old lady doing it for a fit young chap like me...

What on earth had I looked like

to provoke such concern? I don't limp; I do have a tendency to shuffle absent-mindedly sometimes, but I can easily stop shuffling when I realise I am doing it. I vaguely remember hearing that hesitant walking is a symptom of something fairly dire... can't remember what. Death, probably. Any free diagnosis and advice, Dr Stuttaford?

Does Argos sell gym equipment? Rejuvenating running machines, horizontal bars, heavy weights for lifting (mind your bad back). Makes me tired to think of it all. Better have another glass of red and get to bed.

Old men's hair is an oddity: head hair falls out, leg hair disappears (a little girl once said old men's legs look like celery), whereas nose and ear hair sprouts forth in abundance. Why? If it's not too personal a question, what happens to oldie lady hair? Obviously, no baldness, no nose hair, no ear hair, but does it fountain forth elsewhere? Answers on a postcard, please. All correspondence treated in strictest confidence, but no photographs, thank you.

This Argos drama took place on the 18th September, exactly four months to the day before 18th January, when the great EIGHT-OH comes crashing in. Eighty!!!

Kiddies in their thirties have a horror of the looming FOUR-OH when they feel LIFE comes to an end, but really it is only YOOF that comes to an end.

So what comes to an end at 80? Yoof is long gone, middle age long gone, redundancy, retirement, pension, all in the past. So what's going to go next? Not much left to go, is there?

Still, that's LIFE, innit? Only LIFE left to go.

"Got inny powst?"

OH DEAR! OUR poor old Royal Mail. The rot set in with the decline of the postmark. Turning out a cupboard in my parents' house, I came across a drawer full of letters I'd written home during two years of National Service. Just think – a teenager writing a letter! The fifty-year-old postmarks were as clear as if printed yesterday: CATTERICK CAMP 3.15 pm TUES 23 SEPT 1957. Times were marked in quarter hours.

Today, here in the Sussex countryside, the smudged and almost illegible postmarks say Gatwick or Sussex Coast. What is that supposed to mean?

Sherlock Holmes used to get half a dozen deliveries every day, often receiving letters on the day they were posted. Postmen wore uniforms with caps, badges and shiny boots. They were probably inspected before they were allowed to start delivering. After all, they were servants of the Sovereign and were carrying the Royal Mail.

Yesterday, I saw a small red van stopping just across the road.

"Oh good," I thought. "The post." An obese woman emerged, greasy blonde rats-tails hung down her back over a baggy, red T-shirt, her denim skirt flapped round her fat, bare legs and she wore soft blue boots like old ladies' zip-up slippers.

"No, it's not the post," I thought. Then she turned and I saw she was holding an armful of letters. "Ye Gods! It *is* the post. That poor creature is a *postman*" – or postperson, as PC now dictates.

Then, only last week at the dentist when they were processing my card for the usual astronomical payment, there burst in an archetypal football hooligan. Shaven head, stubble, rings in nose, lip and ears, tattooed neck, T-shirt plastered with sports insignia, shorts with yet more stripes and flashes, hairy tattooed legs and huge white trainers.

This ape grunted "Got inny powst?" and one of the two ladies behind the desk handed him a pile of mail. He grabbed it without a word and blundered out, leaving the door wide open.

"Haven't seen *him* before,"' said one lady to the other. "Nor have I," came the reply. "So how do you know he *was* a postman?" I asked, suppressing a scream.

The two ladies looked at one another, silent and bemused. I was bemused too, but also incandescent.

But never mind the Royal Mail; if the same ever happens to the Royal Navy, then we are all doomed. Aye. Doomed.

ART SNOBBERY

SNOBBERY IN THE arts is endemic and there is a clear hierarchy.

At the top is Opera: posh people in posh places and, despite massive tax payer support, more than any other art form, it is still stupendously expensive. Who can afford to go? Only posh people.

Next rung down is The Theatah, darling. Just count the knighthoods. Again, how many go? And who are they? The majority of theatre-goers are white, middle class and middle-aged. They're now having to give away tickets to the under-25s, to lure them in.

Below Theatre comes Literature, though it took many decades for the novel to become respectable and not just an entertainment for housemaids. Hovering uncertainly in the background is Poetry. Neither Larkin nor Auden was honoured, though Betjeman was, possibly as much for his television as his verse.

Next below is Painting. Not many knighthoods there. Stanley Spencer had to wait till he was an OAP and Francis Bacon got nothing, but then, he drank and was Irish.

Sculpture also hovers in the background, rather like Poetry, but makes more of an impression because it is big, heavy and difficult to move. So we have Sir Henry Moore and Dame Barbara Hepworth.

Below Painting comes Illustration. Oh, dear. The very word is used as a pejorative. The worst thing you can say about a painting is that it is "illustrative". If the painter hears you, he will kill you. This, despite the world-renowned names of John Tenniel, Beatrix Potter, and E. H. Shepard.

Below them comes Cartoons. Here we are virtually in the gutter press, despite Carl Giles and David Low. Admittedly, he eventually became Sir David Low. No doubt the government was trying to butter up the proprietor.

Then, below the gutter, are the sewers – Strip Cartoons! Comics! Ugh! The very cesspits of non-culture, read by utterly common people such as children, foreigners and Americans.

On the continent, Bande Dessinée is a respected medium, just as important as Theatre and Film. They call it Ninth Art. In Japan, Manga are published in their millions.

Now, at last, the Graphic Novel has attained dignity and respect in this country. Thanks mainly to Jonathan Cape, Britain is at last waking up to this centuries-old art form.

Recently, there was a presentation about the Graphic Novel at the I.C.A. Soon there is to be a similar event at the Royal Society of Literature. Steven Spielberg wants to make a multimillion dollar movie of Tintin. Both Ian Rankin and Philip Pullman are writing for the medium.

Respect! About time, too.

Where's the MONEY?

Bag and baggage

YESTERDAY, TO MY dismay, I found myself reading a fashion column. Me? Fashion? The grandchildren would fall about. Nevertheless, this was not just the usual feminine fancies; this was serious stuff about bags, well worthy of the attention of a mature, intellectual male.

I have never understood the reluctance of most men to have a bag. They seem to think it is effeminate. I cannot see how anyone can live without one. A woman without a bag is unthinkable. Just think – Thatcher – bagless! So, why is it almost unthinkable for a man to have one? To me they are essential. Do you really want to carry all that stuff in your pockets? And now that fewer men are wearing jackets, it all has to go into trouser pockets. This is why so many oldie men are seen wearing those anglers' waistcoats with pockets all over.

A young friend of mine, a kid in his fifties, often asks me: "What do you keep in that blessed bag you lug about everywhere and won't be parted from?"

"My life!" I say. It's all there, in the bag. So stand by, folks! All is to be revealed. Here we go! Ready for your derision. Black shoulder bag, 15" x 11", nylon fabric, seven zipped pockets, cost £9 a year ago. Made in China, where else?

1. Back pocket: wallet with cheque book and emergency cash £100, plastic magnifier 6" x 2", two paying-in books, cheques to be paid in.

2. Big document pocket, with internal net and elastic straps: rarely used as I have few important documents in old age.

3. Main pocket: wallet with all cards other than bank cards – RA, Tate, Art Fund, Sussex Wildlife Trust, Soc Authors, South Downs Soc, Royal Soc Lit, Brighton Polytechnic Library! (Ye Gods! slightly out of date, it's been a uni for over 20 years), RAC, Uni of London Alumni, Alzheimer's Fund, Cartoon Museum... weighs nearly half a pound (yoof: 190 gms), all used once in a blue moon, most of them never. Two cases of off-the-peg glasses, wedge to stop café tables wobbling, Woolworth's zipped superman pencil case with sharp knife, nail clippers and file, tape measure and scissors. Small folding mirror.

4. Important pocket: wallet with cash, usual bank cards, spare car key, cards for Senior Rail, Tesco, Virgin Phone GIMME SOME CREDIT (how frightfully common – yoof again), purse for coins, case with new glasses, case with new hearing aids (rarely used).

5. Small pocket: driving or TV glasses, phone numbers book.

6. Small pocket meant for phone: used for miniature hair brush (miniature hair).

7. Pocket with mobile instructions: headphones (never used) and Virgin GIMMe card, again!

This leaves notebook, pen, pencil, diary, phone and handkerchief to go into clothes pockets. Glasses hung round neck. Keys on chain fastened to belt.

A yoof might say: "Wotchoo goddallat flippinstuffor, eh?" And, yes, Ai think that the fellow may hev a point. Ai may be overdoin' it slately. (It weighs over fave pounds.) It's all due, don't y'know, to Old Age Anxiety.

Burning embarrassment in wartime

IN 1940 I had been evacuated from London and was living in a cottage in Dorset with two old ladies, Auntie Flo and Auntie Betty. Years later, I realised that these ladies were not old at all, but were in their early forties. Born about the turn of the century, they were two of the many thousands of "spinsters" created by the slaughter in the First World War. They would have been about eighteen in 1918. Not a good time to be on the look-out for a young man.

Once, when playing in the garden, I lost a favourite toy. It was a little pig in grey trousers and a black frock coat, about two inches high. It was made of lead and painted with gloss paint.

I had bought it only a week or two before and it had cost sixpence. I was very upset by the loss and even cried. Kind Auntie Flo said she would buy me another toy to replace it when we went into

Shaftesbury on the weekly bus.

On the Saturday she gave me the new toy, which cost fourpence. I can remember walking along the pavement beside her, looking down at the paving stones passing under my feet and wrestling with my conscience. Even today, when visiting Shaftesbury, I can re-live the dreadful moment by walking over the same pavement and remembering my unforgiveable words: "You owe me tuppence."

I knew at the time that it was wrong. I was burning with embarrassment, yet I had to say it. It is even more embarrassing and shameful today, as I now know how poor they were. Neither was at work, both had been in service all their lives, and their mistress in her will had left them a tiny pension. Betty had inherited the cottage from her uncle. So, in some ways, they were quite fortunate.

But then to have this evacuee dumped on them – though they were probably pleased to have me, a nephew, a nice, well-behaved little boy from Wimbledon Park, rather than having some common brat from Bermondsey billeted on them.

Mercifully, I can't remember what Auntie Flo's reaction was. What a mean, materialistic greedy, ungrateful, selfish, unimaginative, unfeeling, self-pitying, money-grubbing little five-year-old blighter I must have been.

Today, of course, I am quite different.

Socialising: why make a meal out of it?

DINNER PARTIES. GOD spare us. Did we ever do them, once upon a time? Yes, we did. Why? Did we really enjoy them? Or was it just a habit, an obligation, almost a duty?

Nowadays, they are unthinkable. When Liz and I sit on the sofa, semicomatose after our evening meal, and I am wondering if it's worth heaving myself off the cushions to flog all the way across the room to get the *Radio Times*, I sometimes say to Liz: "Do you realise that this is arriving time? Any moment now, six people would come smiling in, bearing wine, gifts and flowers." "Oh, don't," she says weakly. We would all then chatter drunkenly 'til midnight and beyond. Also, in those days, the room would be choked with smoke. It still stank when we staggered down in the morning to face the mountain of washing-up.

Insanity. Does any oldie still practise this lunatic ritual? Do the young still do it? Those under 60, I mean.

First would come The Planning... who would go with whom... better be careful... wasn't she having a bit of a go with him? Did her husband know? No, but his wife did. Better leave it...

Then, The Date... endless phoning to find a time when eight people were all free on the same evening.

Then, The Recipes... no, we can't do that, this lot have had it before... no, not that, Angela's done it twice... and she's brilliant at it... (there was always a slight air of competition).

Then came The Shopping... for weird ingredients we'd never heard of.

Then, oh spare us, The Cooking... anxiety... nervous tension... rows... divorce?

When we were really young – students and twenties – an evening meal with friends was a treat. Gosh! A bottle of wine! And a foreign recipe! (Elizabeth David, Penguin, 2/6d!) Spaghetti not out of a tin. Oh, really? It's called pasta, is it?

Then later, in middle age, everyone was eating in restaurants all the time, usually to do with work, so it was no longer a treat to have fancy foreign food.

Many years ago, I wrote to all our friends saying that, due to increasing decrepitude, would they mind if we dropped the dinner-party habit, and suggested we meet for tea instead, as the main point of any gathering was the people, not the food.

It's so long ago now, I can't remember what became of the idea. We certainly stopped giving dinner parties. Can't remember the teas either... but then even tea parties are rather tiresome, aren't they?

Perhaps we're getting old.

The daftness of ideas about class and the idiocies of education

IN 1956, A fellow student at the Slade was David Storey, later to become a renowned novelist and playwright. It was a great shock to me when I learned that he was a rugby player. What was even more amazing was that he was a professional rugby player. Every weekend in the season he would go up to Yorkshire to play for Wakefield Town.

I was astounded by this. I thought Sport and Art were at opposite poles. Artists were meant to be gentle, sensitive beings, leaning towards the feminine side of their natures, whereas sporting oafs were thugs.

Not only was it sport, but it was rugby, the thing I hated most at school. All that barging into other sweaty people, sticking your head between other blokes' bums in the scrum, all that mud. Then the horrors of the communal bath, with ten or more naked idiots horsing about in a few inches of filthy, tepid water.

How could an artist do that? I was even more astonished when David told me he went to the dogs. The dogs! Common people went to the dogs: uneducated, unintelligent, non-artists. Not only was it a so-called sport, but it was lower class as well. Artists were meant to be educated middle class, weren't they? Otherwise what was all our education for? Once again, I was bewildered.

Someone told me that John Berger, the great left-wing *New Statesman* art critic, was forming a Northern Young Artists group and asked if he had approached me. I said no, he hadn't, but even if he had, Wimbledon Park might have weakened my case for joining. This was about the time when being Northern and working class was becoming fashionable and even glamorous. Would Wimbledon Park ever become fashionable and glamorous?

One of the few student paintings I remember from the Slade at that time was by David Storey. It was a formless splurge of greens, and stretched across it from one screw to another was a green metal spring. It was called *Spring Landscape*.

For 1956 it was years ahead of its time and probably showed what David Storey thought of the art world.

Years later at Brighton, there was a similar joke by a Fine Art student. The time came for the Degree Show, in which every student puts up an exhibition of their work, ready for assessment. This wag put all his work in a sealed plastic bag with instructions that it was not to be opened. He couldn't be given a grade as no assessor had seen the work. On the other hand, he couldn't be failed, for the same reason. So he passed with a Third and is now a Bachelor of Art with Honours.

And of course the Art School, like everywhere else today, is a "Uni".

Are crisps the new grapes?

RECENTLY, A CASUAL acquaintance introduced me to the corruption of Crisps. It was only about a week ago, yet already I am an addict. They have evening classes for Alcoholics Anonymous, don't they? So why are there no classes for Covert Crisp Crunchers? There should be, because like alcohol, they ease the burden of the struggles in life such as cooking: that tiresome business of having to heat up all those Waitrose ready-meal packets. This is always relieved by a glass or three of wine and now can be further enhanced

by Crisps. They are the perfect accompaniment to the wine: dry, crunchy and salty. And of course, the saltiness makes you need to drink more wine, which is an added bonus.

However, I've already discovered that they do have serious disadvantages and that they are possibly in league with Grapes, working against the common good of humanity. Obviously, Grapes can break bones as mentioned in "The Cussedness of Inanimate Objects" (TCOIO) but Crisps can draw blood. They have already drawn some of mine and we have only just met.

They must have been recruited into TCOIO, as only last night they teamed up with the Brigade of Grapes and launched a full frontal assault. In my innocence, I was happily crunching a couple of Crisps with a nice Chilean white wine, when I felt a needle-like prick on my upper lip. I thought nothing of it and poured another glass. Then I felt a stickiness on my lips and saw red marks on the rim of the glass. What on earth? Next I felt a warm trickle down my chin, so I went to the kitchen mirror and there was Frankenstein's monster gazing, wide-eyed at me – bloody lips, bloody teeth, trickle of blood about to drop off his chin.

Having rinsed and tissued, I examined these infernal Crisps. They are very large, two or three inches across, with very sharp edges. When snapped, they often decide to create a needle point at one corner. Who has trained them to do this? You have to be highly skilled; as an experiment, I tried to do it myself, with no success. It can only be undercover agents of TCOIO. This decided me to look deeper into the lurking danger of Crisps in our community.

So this morning, I went into Waitrose to investigate. There I found that one side of an entire aisle is devoted solely to Crisps! Umpteen different makes, umpteen different flavours: Tortillas, Roasted Red Chilli, Indonesian Cracker, Louisiana Sweet & Smoky, Thai Sweet Chilli, Jalapeno… on and on it goes.

This reminded me of the grandchildren's Crisp-Free School, which recently put out a list of Class A and Class B drugs: Coke, Charlie, Crack, Rock, Stone, E, Brownies, Burgers, Smack, Horse, Gear, Scag… Surely Waitrose could make all this into a nice family outing? The two addictions together in a single aisle? Grannie and Grandad on one side absorbed in Crisps, while the grandchildren go trotting along all the Uppers, Jellies, Moggies, Mazzles, et cetera. All this might help to ease the Generation Gap. Gap? Is that Class A or Class B? I must ask the grandchildren. Hi Kids! Got any Gap?

Name-dropping

IT IS STRANGE that ordinary trade names can hold such a place in *The Oldie* mind. They have almost the same resonance as nursery rhymes and, like the rhymes, they are part of our memory and our childhood: Golden Syrup, Bourneville Cocoa, Robinson's Lemon Barley Water, Horlicks, Fyffes, Oxo, Saxa, Tizer, Typhoo Tea, and even Vim.

I suppose it is only nostalgia, which, we are told, is bad for us, but it doesn't mean we idealise these products – "Wasn't life wonderful then?" – it is simply that

they are part of memory and are still in our minds today.

Mum's Hoover, our battered, brown Thermos for picnics on the common, the Pyrex kept under the dresser, my dad polishing our brass stair rods with Bluebell. The home-made wooden box of shoe-cleaning stuff kept under the draining board with tin after tin of Cherry Blossom. Mum's Brownie box camera, Kodak, and Dad's Rolls Razor. Hovis, Liquorice Allsorts, Quality Street, Golden Shred...

The fact that these names have been around for so long gives us a sense of continuity and security. Rowntree's Dairy Box, Black Magic, Lifebuoy – even Rinso, Persil and Lux.

Many of these names are now multinationals, but it doesn't seem to matter; they still touch us. So much so, that when Alliance took over Boots, they changed their own name to Boots. Probably because it had been around for decades and was held in some affection by everyone.

This is why it was such a shock when Woolworth's disappeared. It had been part of all our childhoods – the Threepenny and Sixpenny Store, used by generation after generation. If Woolworth's could go, anything could go, even the Empire, but then that had gone already, like Rinso.

Camp Coffee with its kilted Army officer being waited on respectfully by his humble, turbanned Indian servant. Oh, dear.

At our local Woolworths branch it was quite upsetting to see its doors closed, its windows blanked out, the gold letters taken down from the fascia, leaving the ghostly, grey shadows of the lettering still readable.

One old lady looking up at it had tears in her eyes.

Switching camps

SIR: It seems that, when he wrote "Namedropping", Raymond Briggs missed the fact that the "kilted Army officer being waited on respectfully by his humble, turbaned Indian servant" who once appeared on our bottles of Camp Coffee, has recently managed to regularise the situation.

These days the two of them are shown sitting together, each with his cup of CC, deep in companionable conversation – the latest news from Helmand, perhaps?

Michael Stokes, Biddenden, Kent

The ghost of Christmas past

FAMILIES: SUCH A wonderful thing, aren't they? Everyone loves the idea of The Family, and yet, everyone takes it for granted. It is often forgotten that many people have no family at all.

By the time you are in your seventies, the entire generation above you – father, mother, aunts, uncles, grandparents – is long gone. Then, if you are an only child, you have no brothers or sisters, so you cannot become an aunt or an uncle. Also, if you have not had children yourself

you cannot become a grandparent or even an in-law. You have no family whatsoever. Occasionally, there may be the odd cousin somewhere, whom you have not seen for decades and hear of only by Christmas cards.

Ah, Christmas! Such a happy family time. The merry throng gathered round the tree and the turkey, all together in love and Christmas joy.

A friend of mine has three daughters, all in their forties, so he has three sons-in-law and seven grandchildren. This Christmas, his sister and her husband came, so there were seventeen people staying over Christmas. Not my idea of joy, but marginally better than being alone, perhaps.

These thoughts were prompted by the recent death of my dear cousin, who was almost a sister to me, possibly because she, too, was an only child. She was eighty years old.

There is another, even older cousin, whom I have not seen for over half a century. Her Christmas card is the only proof that she still exists.

So that's my "family", folks! One cousin! Season of Great Joy! I might have a big family get-together, if she can come. Hire a hall, or something...

Fortunately for me, my partner Liz has a lovely family (eighteen people in all) who make us welcome and give us a wonderful Christmas Day.

So in moments of seasonal piety, I still try and spare a thought for the thousands of old people who are not so lucky and have no one. Not a soul.

Here Endeth my First Sermon.

IS YOUR JOURNEY REALLY NECESSARY?

TRAVEL SICKNESS. WHY is the whole world suffering from it?

British Airways goes on strike. Major crisis! No planes for two whole weeks. Whatever shall we do? The fact that there are dozens of other airlines polluting the skies and choking the airports doesn't seem to be relevant.

Yesterday a friend told me his granddaughter had to be at school that morning at 4 A.M.! She must have been dragged out of bed at 3 A.M. Why? Travel, of course. The school was taking a herd of children to COLOGNE, would you believe? Why on earth Cologne? We used to bomb it in the War, didn't we? There can't be much left to see, surely? Further more, they were going by COACH! In the depths of winter with eight inches of snow all over the country. Needless to say, they got stuck on the motorway and had to give up. They were back by lunch time having endured nine hours of misery. Why did they not stay at home, sit by the fire and read an improving book?

Still worse, a neighbour told me that he had recently taken his little boy to see Father Christmas in Lapland.

I assumed he meant a "Lapland" in a department store in Tunbridge Wells, but no, he meant the real life Lapland in Finland, north of the Arctic Circle! They left Gatwick at 7A.M. and were back in time for tea.

I give up. It's beyond words.

Though the very word "travel" says it all. It comes from the French *travail*: painful or laborious effort.

My parents, born about 1900, knew little about travel. Apart from the annual holiday in Bognor or Littlehampton, they went nowhere and were quite happy about it.

Has travel made the world a happier place today? Or is it just more and more *"travail"*?

Besides, what about Greenery and Carbon Footprints? In the War there were posters everywhere asking: IS YOUR JOURNEY REALLY NECESSARY? What a good idea.

Bring back the War, when the world was sane!

The times

WHAT DIFFERENT TIME worlds we all live in!

My world is mainly in book publishing, so an editor might phone me and say: "We're going to do a new catalogue soon, so could you write a couple of hundred words on... ?" "Yes, I say, when do you want it?" "Oh, end of the month all right?"

Then, perhaps a gallery or museum might ask a similar question, and if I ask when, they say: "Oh well, it'll be next summer, so... early April?"

Once I was phoned by a daily newspaper: "We're doing an obituary on... Would you like to contribute about 150 words?" "Oh yes, very pleased. When do you want it?"

"Five o'clock? WHAT! TODAY?" "Yes," he said, sounding slightly bewildered. "Well," I said, "it's ten to one now, I've got to go out this afternoon. I can do it this evening and send it tomorrow morning. An obituary needs a bit of thought." A long sigh... "Very well – nine o'clock." "Er, could you make it ten? I have to get the dog out." A groan... "OK, ten."

Next day, on the stroke of ten, he phoned. I said, "I'll fax it." "No, don't fax it. Dictate it." "Oh blimey," I said, "I've never done that." Then he went on: "Can you let us have a CV?" "Oh, er yes, OK... When? " "Well, it'll take me a minute to connect you to the dictation, so..." "WHAT! you mean NOW? Instantly?" So I had barely sixty seconds to write my life story.

At the art school we used to have "crits" (criticisms) first thing in the morning. "First thing" for art students is 10 o'clock. The day officially started at 9:30, late enough, but it would have been useless to have a crit at that time. No one would be there.

Once you'd got to know the new bunch of students, you could write out a list of the times they would arrive. Group 1 arrived before time, pinned up their work and sat waiting. Group 2 would rush in apologetically, just in time. Group 3 would hurry in, slightly late, but unbothered. Group 4 strolled in casually, very late and almost insolent in manner. Group 5 didn't turn up at all. Each group was always composed of exactly the same people.

Then recently, there was a bit on the TV news which gave me the shudders: some huge delay with the 2.47 A.M. (!) train from Margate. Freezing East Coast, miles of grey sea stretching to Scandinavia, icy winds... And quarter to three in the morning! Margate! I'd rather die.

I used to collect the shopping for a housebound 87-year-old lady, and one day on the phone, she was getting in a slight muddle. "Oh dear," she said. "I'm so sorry... I'm not at my best first thing in the morning..." (it was twenty-five past ten.) then, another day, she asked me: "What time does the shop open? Half past nine?" "Er... no, I said. Quarter past five."

Now, even that is a bit too early for me. Still, it's better than Margate at quarter to three.

Bribery and lies

POLICE CORRUPTION? THE Press telling lies? So what's new? My old dad was corrupting the police in 1946. He told me about it when we were out on his milk round, soon after he had done it. I was twelve at the time.

There had been a slight collision between his milk van and another vehicle. No one was hurt and there was very little damage, but someone had called the police.

A bobby rolled up on his bike and took notes from the other bloke, who soon drove off. Then the bobby started taking notes from Dad, and in the midst of this, he pointed to the crate of milk on the nearside floor of the driver's cab. There were no doors, the cab was open and all the milkmen kept a crate there as it was easy and quick to get at. "That shouldn't be there," said the bobby. "No, right. OK, mate," said Dad. After writing a bit more, the bobby said: "I'll have to mention it in the report. It's illegal." "Yeah, right," said Dad.

After a third mention of the crate, my father realised what was going on. So, when finally the bobby asked for his licence, Dad had put a ten bob note in it. This disappeared without another word being said, and later there was no mention of the crate in the report.

The Press lying? Putting words into people's mouths? Words they had never spoken and if they *had* spoken as reported, it would have made *them* liars.

My mum had the Press putting lies into her mouth in 1931. She had just won the crossword competition in the *People*: £100! Worth about a million in today's money. The *People* trumpeted: "Mrs Briggs was overjoyed. She told us: 'This £100 will at last pay off our mortgage!'"

Far from paying it off, their mortgage had scarcely begun. It took them another twenty-four years to pay off the colossal sum of £850.

Such sin in South London! Earlsfield and Wimbledon Park in the 1940s – what festering pits of depravity they must have been! Chicago? New Orleans? The Bronx? Peanuts. And furthermore, the corrupt Clapham Junction, so dangerously close and still in the grip of that notorious pair, Arding & Hobbs.

Why bottle maid's water?

NEVER WRITE FOR *The Oldie*. Everything you send in will be translated into teenagetextspeak.

Almost all your punctuation will be altered or cut out. No capitals are allowed, except at the beginning of a sentence, no colons, semi-colons, brackets, quotation marks or small caps, but worst of all, particularly in speech, no italics and no ellipses. (Juvenile delinquents who have never heard of an ellipsis can look it up on wickiwotsit.) BRACKETS, PLEASE.

For months, I've been going to do a Rant about it but, it seemed rude and disloyal. But, last week in desperation I phoned the editors (who are always helpful and charming, CREEP CREEP. SMALL CAPS, PLEASE.) to find out why there is this crippling house style.

It turns out that it is all due to our old friend, The Computer. Every article received goes into a programme called designit. *[Surely InDesign? Ed.]* So the computer writes the piece as much as its author. It should be called designitsh*t. The oaf who designed this so-called programme is obviously illiterate.

The Le Carré novel I am reading at the moment uses italics time and again in the *text*, ITALICS PLEASE, not just in speech where it is essential. Take the famous American phrase: "I should buy two tickets for her concert?" Try saying it aloud emphasising a different word each time. Every utterance will have a different meaning.

Another de-humanising computerisation has recently invaded our doctor's Reception. You no longer go up to the desk, say good morning and introduce yourself to the receptionist, who smiles and says good morning. No, now you have to report to a screen-thing which displays the months of the year: TOUCH THE MONTH OF YOUR BIRTH, commands the gadget. Up then comes the alphabet: TOUCH THE INITIAL LETTER OF YOUR SURNAME, it says. Then up comes... ELLIPSIS PLEASE. Never mind, too boring.

After all this inhumanity, it was a relief to come across some good old-fashioned dottiness. I had gone along the lane to post a letter in the small Victorian box which is set deep into the hedge.

On top of the box, amidst the twigs and leaves, there was a small glass bottle. I took it out and saw it was almost full of a clear, yellow liquid. A handwritten label on the side said MAIDS WATER.

This was slightly strange in Sussex commuter-land, ten minutes' walk from a main line station with frequent trains to Victoria. It's not exactly Cold Comfort Farm country with Starkadders prowling round the hedgerows.

What sort of person uses the word "maid"? How old are they? No child or teenager would use the word. It almost certainly was not Maids Water, so why pretend it was? Why bottle it? Why put it in the hedge? Who was meant to find it?

Ada Doom saw something nasty in the woodshed. Did she put something nasty on the post box? If she did, then good old Aunt Ada. She cheered me up no end.

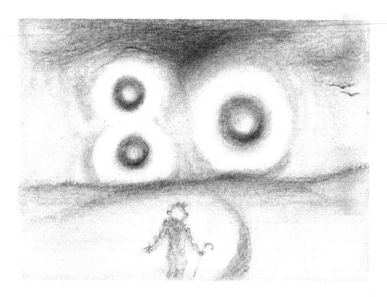

The dawn of darkness

AS THE DREAD eight-oh looms on the not-too-distant horizon, thoughts inevitably turn to Residential Hotels, Retirement Homes, Nursing Homes and similar places, such as prisons and lunatic asylums.

These institutions all pretend to be nice to you, except the last two perhaps, but however polite, charming and even subservient they may appear to be, the moment you enter, they are in charge of you. They are the boss and you are under their control.

We once became friends with an ex-Army officer living in a nearby retirement hotel. He was fit and well, tall, strong and still under seventy, but now widowed and having come from a background of nannies, cooks, servants and batmen, he could not possibly look after himself. He was the very embodiment of the "couldn't boil an egg" brigade. We came to know his hotel quite well and even went to his seventieth birthday lunch there – a lunch with the smallest portions I have ever seen on a plate.

These hotels are very strict about not being care homes. The moment you need "care" you will be asked to leave. This is understandable, though it must be a blow to the resident. But when does everyday concern become "care"? Giving an old lady an arm when she climbs the stairs? You would not routinely do that in a hotel, so how often do you have to do it before you become a "carer"?

Another danger lurks: if someone is frail and a little vague, the hotel people can "help" them with their affairs – tax, investments, etc., particularly if the person has no surviving family. The people who ran this hotel befriended a ninety-one-year-old guest and even took her on holiday with them. Who paid for these cruises, no one knows, but when she died she left them her entire fortune. So, even if they had paid for the holidays, it wasn't a bad investment.

The other day I came across something I wrote about the hotel at the time. It is meant to be humorous, but apart from the motto, every word is true.

HOTEL GUIDE

ROOMS: all rooms are routinely sprayed with deodorant to remove smells of smoking, dogs, and guests.

GARDEN: guests are requested to refrain from feeding wild birds so as to ensure that the lawns may remain free of any unpleasantness. Similarly, squirrels are discouraged so that guests are not frightened by their sudden appearance on windowsills.

DINING: to ensure variety in the menus, kitchen staff are closely supervised and replaced at monthly intervals. Should the need arise, special arrangements can be made for guests who wish to remove slices of bread from their tables.

SECURITY: whenever an emergency occurs, such as a pint of milk being mislaid, a thorough search is instituted at once and all guests are closely questioned.

TOILET: a certain amount of toilet paper is freely available on request.

OUR MOTTO IS: Ever serve you right.

* P.S. Before delivering yourself into one of these places, it is advisable, if at all possible, to find out whether or not the proprietors are barmy.

Mum!
What have I got to wear
red, white and blue
to school for?
        Because it's Empire Day.
What's empire?

Do keep
STILL!

Empire Day and all that

WHEN YOU GET well into Old Age and look back at your childhood, you realise you were born in a remote historical time. Everyday memories of that time now sound antique or picturesque.

I remember my mother unpacking the box of weekly groceries Dad had just brought in from the Co-op. She looked at the bill and let out a cry of anguish: "No! Oh, no! Look at that! It's over a POUND!" Today our weekly grocery bill from Waitrose is usually around £180. Mind you, my parents had never heard of wine.

Our baker's roundsman had a long stick like a broom handle with a right-angled, six-inch spike at one end. With this he would reach into his large, horse-drawn van and hook down a loaf from a high shelf. Unwrapped, of course. GIs over here were forbidden from eating our grubby British bread. There were horse-drawn delivery carts everywhere: milk, bread, greengrocery, flowers, coal, beer...

Hitler always liked to keep quiet about his Blitzkrieg army being almost wholly dependent on horse transport. It didn't quite go with the Master Race image.

There were so many horses that housewives would scurry out into the street with buckets to shovel up the steaming droppings before their neighbours got there first.

The narrow cul-de-sac, where my father was born, was gradually taken over by costermongers. Dozens of up-ended carts were parked outside their houses; I remember seeing the shafts pointing to the sky like a forest of masts. The horses were kept in the back yards, and as there were no back entrances they had to be led through the living rooms and kitchens.

But there were some motor deliveries, too. Just round the corner from us a yellow lorry was often parked, filled with huge blocks of ice under a green canvas cover. As kids we used to reach inside and chip off bits of ice to eat.

As no one had central heating, everyone had coal delivered. Coalmen wore leather skull caps with a long leather flap at the back, almost down to the waist. Even then they looked almost medieval, and are now probably in museums.

Dustmen also had lorries – dust carts they were called, but with an engine. There were no plastic bin bags, so rubbish was dumped into the bin loose; sticky, smelly and attractive to flies and rats. Dustmen carried containers like Vim cartons and they would shake a pink powder into every emptied bin.

Rag-and-bone men with horses and carts came down our street almost every day, calling: "RAH-BOH, RAH-BOH." Also, there was often a deranged down-and-out who shuffled along the middle of the road chanting in a loud monotone: "Yes, Jesus loves you... yes, Jesus loves you..."

The next street parallel to ours was the boundary between Surrey and London. The southern side had electric street lights and the London side had gas lamps, which now sounds almost Dickensian.

There was so much street life then; goal posts and cricket stumps chalked on end-of-terrace walls, butcher boys, chimney sweeps, and ice cream salesmen were all on bikes with huge boxes on the front. Other forms of transport were slightly different, too. Lorries had plates on the back saying 20 m.p.h. Twenty! If only! Riding our bikes home from school, we would use them as wind cover, pedalling along a few feet behind them. Often, we would hang on with one hand and get a free tow.

At home, one of my domestic jobs was cutting up the salt. This was sold in large blocks, the size of a couple of bricks. You started at one end, shaving off the salt with a bread knife and working slowly along the block.

At school every year, there was "Empire Day". Empire? What was that all about? I've heard of it, of course.

Painters with plaits

WE OLDIES ARE always grumbling about the blows to our self-esteem that come with age, but looking through old notebooks, I realise that just as many blows are suffered in youth.

In the fifties, most of us provincial art students dreamed of one day going on to the Royal College of Art or the Slade School. These were regarded as the Oxford and Cambridge of the art world. So it was galling to arrive at last in this Paradise, particularly after the agonising wait of two years in the Army, to find that the Principal of the Slade, William Coldstream, believed in having a mixture of different types of student. His recipe was to take one-third old lags like me, who had already served four years, one-third students who had already done two years, and horror of horrors, one-third school children. I had worked and waited for six years to gain this privilege. I was now nearly 22, and these children had just strolled into the Slade a few weeks after leaving school.

So you might find yourself working next to some daffy schoolgirl who really did have plaits and was wearing what looked like a blue gingham school frock. Or even worse, a teenage Etonian in a striped tie, smoking a pipe to show how grown up he was, and who actually said "What? What?" at the end of his sentences.

So much for the dreaming spires of Gower Street.

Then it was even more galling to discover that the daffy schoolgirl, still wearing her white ankle socks, was a really good painter, much better than I was. Furthermore, she did it with the casual ease of someone who was blissfully unaware of the difficulties. She would come in, draw in the outlines as easily as if she was tracing a photograph, then paint in the shapes with one coat as if filling in a children's colouring book. There was no struggle, no correcting. Nothing was altered or re-painted and the buggering thing was brilliant.

Didn't she know the problems, or didn't she care? Little cow.

The appian way

THERE IS A new app! Have you heard about it? Fantastic! You can now get an app that will open your front door – without a key! Just think what a relief that will be. When friends come to stay and you want to let them come and go as they please, you don't have to give them a key! They just put your app into their phones! No need to worry about them losing your precious spare key.

It's all quite easy, too. You just need an iPhone which has a Bluetooth wireless facility, and this will provide the e-key. You replace your old ironmongery lock with an electronic one. Then, as you approach your door, the lock will recognise you, and when you touch the door it will open!

It makes life so simple, doesn't it? Then the other day I was walking along the road here when one of our neighbours, Sally, drove past me and stopped outside her house. She reversed into the driveway and I thought I'd say Good Morning in a minute, as it was only fifty yards away. But when I got to the entrance there was no car, no Sally – nothing. All had disappeared in less than a minute or two. I gazed into her empty garden bewildered, almost stunned. Then, at that moment, the side door of the garage opened and she came out. "Sally!" I cried. "How on earth did you do that? You drove past me and two minutes later you had vanished off the face of the earth – car and all!"

Despite being an elderly lady, Sally explained the technology to my failing elderly brain. She has a gadget in the car (obviously containing an app) which, as she reverses up the driveway, automatically opens the up-and-over door of the garage, and, when inside, closes the door again.

Presumably it then opens the side door. Her phone app will open her front door, of course, but how does she get there from the garage without an app? Is this elderly lady expected to walk? It's nearly twenty yards! Suppose it was wet? Suppose the path was icy? Surely there must be an Elderly Lady Anti-Icy app?

As I know nothing about these app things, I'm forced to wonder if we've got one on our water filter jug. You're supposed to change the filter every month, so on top of the lid is a small, black rectangle. When you put in a new filter, you have to press this rectangle; numbers then run by at lightning speed and you press to stop it when it shows the number you want. But it's moving so fast I can never stop it in time, so I give up. I just write the date in felt tip on the lid.

That's another thing about this app piffle – lightning speed. Staying in a hotel last weekend, they had the usual maddening room "keys" that are a bit of plastic card (no doubt with an app concealed in them). Time and again I inserted this key – nothing happened. I tried again and counted eleven times.

Nothing. Eventually, I got the girl receptionist to come and, of course, she did it instantly. When she had gone, I tried again; still no luck. So then I asked a couple of passing residents to help.

Having practised under their direction, I realised I was too SLOW. You have to put the card in as FAST as possible and whip it out again as FAST as possible. BINGO! It works! Lightning speed is the Key to Modern Life wiv Yoof, innit?

Your Resident APPARATCHIK

P.S. HAR! HAR! Sally's car parked outside today. Garage door won't open. TEE! HEE! Apparently app has apped off, no doubt saying app yours.

ESN UNIS

COMPUTERS SEEM TO be destroying literacy. Any imbecile who has learned to type thinks he can write.

I constantly get letters from so-called "students" at so-called "universities" who cannot write even the simplest letter.

They have never heard of terms of address such as Dear Mr or Dear Sir; their letters begin "Hi". There is no address and no date. Sometimes the entire letter is written in texting style with "I" and other capitalized words in lower case throughout. Usually, there is no punctuation whatsoever.

Having typed out this garbage, they then appear to be incapable of reading it through. Maybe they cannot read? One imbecile writes "i would really like a signed of you if possible signed to Michael." He has left out the very thing he is asking for! But, Heaven be praised he has capitalized his own name and put a full stop at the end – the only punctuation on the entire page.

Another halfwit wrote to my agent asking her to forward his letter on to me. Unfortunately, he forgot to mention my name. Luckily, the astute secretary managed to work out who had in mind. He said he was an illustration student and talks about "illustraded books", being an "illustrater" and "storys". He cannot even spell the very subject he is studying! He says he is sending out questionnaires, but at the end he adds a P.S. "sorry i forgot to attach my questionnaire".

Can these cretins really be at UNIVERSITY? If so, the word "university" has lost all its meaning and prestige. No wonder the students themselves prefer to say they are at "uni".

Not a bad word for it.

Years ago there was an unpleasant term, no longer in use – E.S.N. Educationally Sub-Normal.

Maybe it's time to revive it, but to use it now for the institutions, not the people.

Educationally Sub-Normal Universities?

The naked truth

WHY IS NAKEDNESS so powerful? Under the few bits of cloth we put on, we are all naked.

For decades I taught life drawing in an art school. I dealt with naked ladies and gentlemen of all sorts and sizes every day of the week. It was so routine, it was boring. "Would you mind getting changed, please? We'd better make a start." This was the polite way of telling them to get naked.

We even lived through the dramatic change in the early seventies, when, for the first time, the gentlemen were completely naked. Previously, they had worn a little bag on strings which later became known as a "posing pouch". One chap always had a plastic fig leaf stuck on his. Occasionally, an elderly exhibitionist would turn up to flaunt himself in front of the girl students, but he usually provoked more smothered mirth than shock and was soon got rid of.

Then, one evening, an ex-student whom I had worked with for two years came in as a life model. She was already in the changing room when I arrived and a couple of minutes later she stepped out, stark naked.

"Oh, er... hullo, Pauline... er... ah, nice to see you again..." ("Don't look down!" hissed a voice in my head.) But why should I not look down? There was nothing to see, just a patch of fuzzy hair, not attractive, not exciting, not remotely sexy, just a bit of anatomy. We'd all be gazing at it together with her breasts, belly and bum for the next two hours without much interest apart from pencils, charcoal and paper. So what was all the fuss about?

Some time later, a BBC TV producer wanted to talk to me about a programme he was going to make. He could come Monday, Tuesday or Wednesday, and he said he would phone to confirm which day. At the time I had a craze for "naturism" and as the garden is completely private, I sometimes worked in it naked. (I've grown out of it now.) I heard nothing from him again, and so on the Sunday evening I assumed he could not be coming on Monday or I'd have heard.

The following morning I was weeding just outside the open French window when I thought I heard heavy footsteps walking across the bedroom floor. Bloody hell! I thought. Someone is up there! Filled with rage, I rushed across the sitting room to the stairs and cannoned into someone coming in from the front room. We both cried out "oh! oh!" as we bounced back, crimson with embarrassment.

The front door is a stable door and in hot weather, I leave the top half open, the bottom half bolted. This imbecile had arrived after no phone call, did not ring the bell nor did he knock. He simply walked in. When we sprang apart he said "Sorry... so sorry... I've never seen anyone naked before." It seems these BBC producers lead rather sheltered lives. Perhaps they should take up life drawing.

Since writing this, I have read Mavis Nicholson's column with the letter from the grandfather who accidentally came across his daughter-in-law naked. Now she refuses to speak to him. Yet again, the absurd power of nakedness.

You'll feel a slight prick...

Rats and registrars

HAD A NICE little outing this morning: went to the Doc's. When you live alone, it's good to get out of the house and meet people, isn't it? Otherwise it's Radio 4 all day long. Furthermore, at the Doc's, there is someone who is paid to feign an interest in you and who will listen to you talking about yourself for ten whole minutes. Now, that is a rare treat. Where else could you find someone who was willing to do that?

They told me this new doc is "The Registrar". Golly, I thought, that's good; crème de la crème, it sounds almost royal, top-notch.

As I seem to have gone slightly deaf, he took a look at my ears and noticed a tiny bit of hard skin. Oh, that's been there ages, I said, cheerfully. Years. Never think about it. Doesn't hurt, doesn't itch, nothing. Once in a while, I touch it with my finger, it falls off and I forget about it again. Been to the Doc's umpteen times while it's been there and never mentioned it to him. Too trivial. I'd never even seen it, but it felt about the size of a slight nail paring.

"We'd better send you to the dermatologist," said the registrar.

"Really?" I said. "That's a bit heavy, isn't it?" "See what he says," he replied.

The dermatologist – a strong, hearty chap, took a look and said: "Well, we'd better get this off for you now." With that, he drew on a pair of sinister plastic gloves. I was told to lie down on a black plastic bench, where a nurse held my head locked tight in her plastic glove grip. "You'll feel a slight prick," said the dermatologist. "I feel a right prick already," I said, forcing out a brave, cheery joke. Neither of them laughed. He slashed, cut and scraped for what felt like half-an-hour, while the nurse mopped up. "Is it blood?" I enquired politely.

"Some", she said. "Not much."

Eventually, I staggered out to the car and sat trying to calm my nerves after the trauma. Damn! No drink in the car.

I badly needed one after my ordeal and this got me moving. Managed to keep just under the speed limits by iron self-control.

I was then left with a large, flapping plaster stuck halfway around my head.

A week later, when I went back to have the stitches taken out, the dermatologist handed me a document, a single sheet of A4. BBC it said at the top. Oh, good, I thought, it was secretly recorded and it's going to be broadcast, probably on Radio 4. But in my nervous state, I'd misread it, it was BCC, which is slightly different. Not Radio 4 at all, just Basal Cell Carcinoma.

It's also called "a rodent ulcer". Rodent? That's rats, isn't it? Base rats from cells at that. Don't mind being linked to a rat, a fellow vertebrate mammal, but I wish he was a decent chap like Ratty in *The Wind in the Willows*, not someone "base" and from a cell.

I then discovered that this "registrar" is not a superior sort of doc, as I thought, but the exact opposite – an apprentice doc, straight out of medical school, learning to be a GP!

So, I've got a rat-like base disease and am being dealt with by a school-leaver beginner! You can't get much more basic than that, can you?

P.S. Well, yes you can. They also say it is "common". That is the final straw. My mum would have had a fit: common!?

Three chairs!

CHILDHOOD MISCONCEPT-IONS... AND the revelations that follow them. My earliest was: "Three chairs for the King!" Why would he want three chairs? Because he was so important? Or did he just have a big bottom?

Another well-known one which bewildered many of us was: "There is a green hill far away, without a city wall." But why would a green hill have a city wall anyway? I had the image of a smooth, rounded hill with a stone wall running round its base, then having to say to myself: No. No wall. Take wall away. Leave hill alone.

Another revelation came in the infant class in the village school, when I was evacuated. Miss Zillwood said: "This country is an island." An island! How could it be an *island*? I had travelled hours and hours on a charabanc all the way from Wimbledon Park to Stour Provost. It was so long we had to stop halfway for a wee. Then later, we stopped again for a choc ice (Walls, four pence; I liked Lyons best). All that was supposed to be on an *island*? The longest journey of my entire life? I knew the sea was hours and hours away too, I'd been there. It was at a place called Weymouth.

Surely Miss Zillwood knew an island was a little round thing with a tree in the middle and sharks all round? I'd seen pictures of islands, so I knew.

Soon after, I was sitting on a bank in next door's garden arguing with their evacuee – my friend Ron, a tough older boy from Bermondsey. I thought I'd clinched the argument by saying triumphantly: "Well, my aunties say – "

"Yeah?" he said. "So what? Your bloody aunties don't know everything." This struck me like a thunderbolt. I can still remember exactly where we were sitting on the bank in that garden, Ron chewing a stalk of grass as usual. My aunties don't know everything! That meant other grown-ups might not know everything. They could be wrong. Even Miss Zillwood could be wrong. I knew she was wrong about islands.

One day back in London, a friend and I saw a dog and a bitch hard at it; the dog quivering, panting and dribbling with excitement. I'd never seen this before, but knew what they were doing and was quite shocked.

"Your mum and dad do that," said my friend. What a daft thing to say! Of course, I knew it was nonsense, just like the islands.

Yours ever, insincerely

EVERY SO OFTEN something crops up which reminds us oldies that we were born in another age, long gone.

Yesterday, a middle-aged bloke on a TV quiz show was asked how many shillings there were in a guinea. He was baffled, stayed silent, then guessed 25. In the olden days, I always sent out my bills in guineas. It sounded posher. Also, 50 guineas was 52 pounds 10 shillings, so you got more.

The letters went off to the client addressed: John Smith Esq.

Esquire! When did I last write that on an envelope? Today, I don't even write Mr, Mrs or Ms, just the name. The letters began: "Dear Mr Smith", or "Dear Sir". Why do we say dear? Often the person is anything but dear to us. Modern yoof just says hi.

"Dear Sir" will soon become as antique as: "I remain, Sir, your most obedient humble servant". Fifty years ago, this seemed to us bizarre, yet at one time it was customary. My editor always signed off with "Yours Ever", which even then seemed to me to be a bit too lovey-dovey. But we still say "Yours Sincerely". Yours? Am I really his? I hope not. In recent years I've started saying With Best Wishes, as it seems less romantic.

Soon, the handwriting of cheques will also be seen as an outdated, almost quaint custom. A yoof will say: "Wot? you just like write out a bitta paper an like giv it ter sumdee inna shop yeah? Jus spose it ad 10k onnit! The bitta paper is werf 10k innit. Yoo all musta bin menall."

At the Slade School in the fifties there remained an almost Dickensian oddity: the doorman, known as the beadle. He stood in a small cubby hole just inside the door, and had a huge book in which students had to sign in. He wore a long crimson coat with brass buttons and gold braid, and on special occasions a glossy black top hat.

At home, my mother always used to whiten our doorstep by the front gate. This put a fine layer of white powder on the stone. The first person to come through the gate left a perfect footprint in the powder.

So, to protect it she would cover the step with sheets of newspaper. "Mum!" I used to quietly scream at her, "if you're going to cover it with newspaper, why bother to whiten it?"

Another memory is that of visiting my friend Ronnie, in Brixton Prison. He appeared behind a crudely constructed wooden screen, peering out, pale-faced, through a small gap covered in wire mesh. It was like looking at an animal in a hutch. He was still in his twenties, had been mentally ill all his life, and had been convicted of attempted suicide. This had been his second attempt. On his release, he made a third attempt, and succeeded.

Last night, I read of another custom from a bygone age, not much before my time. In the early days of BBC Radio in the 1920s, the newsreader (in dinner jacket, of course) would sometimes say: "I am sorry, but there is no news this evening, so instead I will play a gramophone recording of the Piano Concerto number four by Rachmaninov."

Wonderful! No news. What bliss! A golden age, long gone.

Public and private parts

I ONCE HAD the surreal experience of seeing the same doctor twice in the same year; first in the NHS and later as a private patient.

In the NHS hospital I queued with nine or ten other half-naked blokes in a draughty corridor, waiting to see the surgeon. We shuffled along, whispering nervously to one another, until he called out loudly: 'Next!' I really felt I was back in the Army – Catterick Camp, 1953 and waiting for the notorious Cough Test.*

Eventually, I got into a little bare cubicle of a room with a bed along one wall. "Lie down!" said the great man, so I obediently lay back on the bed. "Left or right?" he barked. "Er... right," I said. He made a mark on my groin with a broad, black felt-tip. "How soon will it be?" I asked. "If it's going to be a long wait, I may go private." "I've no idea," he said, impatiently. "Ask in the office." "Thank you," I said. "Next!" he shouted.

A few months later, long after the operation, I went to see him in his private consulting rooms. These were in a huge house which was part of a grand Regency terrace. A receptionist came to the door and ushered me into the waiting room. This was like a drawing room in a country mansion – tall windows, brocade curtains, sofas, armchairs, a polished antique table with copies of the *Times*, *Country Life*, *Horse* & *Hound* laid out, and a grandfather clock ticking solemnly. There was just one elderly lady reading in an armchair and we nodded silently to one another.

Soon a nurse bustled in and led me into the presence. He came towards me, tall and courtly, saying:

"Hello, Mr Briggs. Let me take your coat." He even hung it up for me. "Do please sit down. Now, how can I help you?"

We were the same two people as before and of course he didn't remember me, but we were still doctor and patient. So, what made the difference? Money, that's all. Money creating class and a pretend respect. He wasn't treating *me* with respect, he was respecting my money.

Golly gosh! I seem to be turning into one of those frightfully common Socialist creatures: WERKERS OF DE WELD UNITE, INNIT!

The Cough Test is when you queue up, naked, and a bloke puts his finger in beside your scrotum and says: "Cough". This should make the testicles move upwards; if it doesn't, they are not connected, and you are unfit to serve your Queen and country.

Shoe a Little Horse

GAMES BRING OUT the worst in people.

We once had a friend who was one of the quietest, gentlest, most sensitive people we had ever met, despite being a journalist and a foreigner. He was kind, considerate, polite and devoted to the green issues, which were his special field.

One Christmas Day, we were playing the game called "Shoe a Little Horse". This I had learned from Big Fat Puffin, the late, great Kaye Webb, chief editor of Puffin Books.

The game is played by clearing the floor and placing a chair at each end of the room. These are the horses. The two competitors are blindfolded and spun round. They then kneel in front of a chair. Eight plastic cups are scattered over the floor.

The competitors have to grope around, on their knees, until they find a cup. They then hasten to the opposite chair, still on their knees, and lift the chair leg to put the chair leg into the cup – shoeing the horse. The winner is the first to get four cups on his horse's legs.

Players often cannot find the opposite chair, or end up shoeing their opponent's chair by mistake, or cannot find a cup at all. They repeatedly barge into one another. Spectators can add to the fun by moving cups out of the way of searching hands or by moving the chairs.

The game is meant for children, but is much better played by over-weight, middle-aged people full of Christmas dinner, wine and brandy.

Our saintly friend was also teetotal, yet when playing this game he turned into a violent maniac. He had to be physically restrained from attacking his opponent.

Even allowing for his foreigner's lack of the British sense of fair play, it was still a shocking incident.

It is truly said that you will learn more about a friend in ten minutes of playing a game with them than you will ever learn in ten years of knowing them.

Anything for a quiet life

I DO LIKE a quiet life. Uneventful as possible, please. Even so, odd things happen.

Almost half a century ago, I became a friend of the great Kaye Webb, founder of Puffin Books, and known affectionately in the trade as Big Fat Puffin.

My wife, Jean, had died in 1973 and Kaye kindly took me under her wing as I had no family, something you desperately need at such a time. My parents had both died in 1971 and I had no brothers or sisters.

We once went to visit her son somewhere out in the wilds of East Anglia. He and his girlfriend were living on a boat moored on a bleak river estuary which seemed to be miles from anywhere. Kaye and I stayed in a hotel some distance away and, one evening we drove over to the boat for a meal. Halfway through the meal, the tide went out and the boat tilted at a crazy angle. This made it difficult to pour a glass of wine or to cope with soup. I suppose sailors get used to this dotty lifestyle, but it's not for me. When I got up to go to the lavatory, I nearly fell over. Nothing to do with the wine of course. And then the lavatory did not flush! With millions of tons of water all around, you'd have thought...

Then later, when we got back to our hotel, we found it closed! In total darkness, not a light anywhere. It was only just after midnight. I groped around the walls in pitch darkness, looking for a back door or a tradesman's entrance, and eventually came to a French window. I tried the handle, it turned and the door swung open. Thank God! We're in!

As I stepped inside, there came a piercing scream, lights flashed on and a man's voice roared: "What the hell do you think you're doing?" An elderly couple were sitting up in bed, glaring at us, the woman still screaming.

"Sorry, so sorry..." I muttered, "Got locked out... sorry... sorry..." Kaye and I backed out of the door, still mumbling apologies.

What on earth were we to do? There was not a light in any of the few buildings in sight. Eventually, we went back to my VW van, not a camper van, just a van, and crawled into it.

Luckily, there was an old duffle coat, and a grubby dog blanket to protect us from the cold, metal floor. Somehow, we got through the night.

When we stormed into Reception in the morning, exhausted, but still fuming, the twerp at the desk was indifferent. "Didn't you see the notice?" he said, pointing casually to a postcard-sized bit of paper: "The Hotel will close at 11:30 P.M. on Saturday 13th October." No one had told us about this, despite passing Reception many times. Why was the notice not put in our rooms? Who had ever heard of a hotel closing at 11:30 P.M.? It makes you want to bring back hanging.

Kaye was over 60 at the time, and an October night spent virtually outdoors, could have had serious consequences for her. Newspaper headlines might have read: "RONALD SEARLE'S EX-WIFE FROZEN IN VAN. A 39-year-old van driver has been arrested." Anything for a quiet life in solitary.

FOOTBALL BORNEO

FOOTBALL. JUST SAY the word and see the faces light up, even girlies. Why has the whole world gone football mad?

The sport has been in existence for centuries, so why now? Once it was the preserve of working class men; now it has become a world religion.

Tribesmen in the wilds of Borneo and the Indonesian jungle support Manchester United. Even the managers and wives of footballers star on television. Top footballers become world fashion "icons", earning millions by lending their names to deodorants and underpants. Their unemployed wives and mistresses spend money in such quantities it is an insult to working people. Apparently, there is even a soap opera on television called *Footballers' Wives*. What next, *Footballers' Babies? Footballers' Mums?*

Bishops in their sermons make football analogies, fortunately not mentioning what position Jesus played – yet. It will come. Melvyn Bragg had to stop a speaker on his radio programme from making a football analogy when discussing philosophy. Three cheers for Lord Bragg. I wonder what team he supports?

Every week *The Times* has a thick supplement entitled "The Game".

"What game?" an innocent might enquire. "Is there only one game?" Yes, there is only one.

TV Sports News, i.e. Football News, is presented by toothy, grinning blonde girlies. This job should be done by old blokes who have been in the business all their lives and know what they are talking about. But of course, they are neither glamorous nor sexy. Anything to do with football must be both.

Any politician hoping to be popular and electable must declare a passion for football, otherwise he doesn't have a hope. Even Tony Blair had to boast about his boyhood devotion to football, claiming to have watched a certain famous player, who in fact had retired years before Blair could have seen him.

Recently, a teenage schoolboy was brutally murdered. The first thing the papers said about him was that he was a promising footballer. More tragic than if he was a mere human being?

The language has become more violent, too. Not long ago the players at the front were called forwards; now they are "strikers". The team is no longer just a team; it is a "squad". Military language.

When something called the World Cup was on, cars drove

around festooned with the flags of St George. Einstein said: "Nationalism is an infantile disease." Judging by the behaviour of English football hooligans on the continent, he was right.

It's lucky these ignoramuses don't know that St George was a foreigner and had his head chopped off by another foreigner.

He must have been supporting the wrong squad.

Oldie angst

IT IS GALLING to be stereotyped, but it is even more galling to find that you *are* a stereotype yourself – the very embodiment of it.

A few years ago I copied this piece from a newspaper. Every single word of it fitted me to a T. Today it fits even more closely. "How do you rate?" it says. Well, I rated Top Hole, a star, Full House, Gold Medal. Bore of the year award.

So, how do *you* rate? Test yourself now. Answers on a postcard, please. Donations to Sussex Stereo Society: Treasurer R. Briggs.

TEN CHARACTERISTICS OF OLD AGE: How do you rate?

1. RIGID IN ADHERING TO ROUTINES OF DAILY LIFE? Can't answer now – four minutes past five! Late for tea.

2. ARE YOUR THOUGHTS TINGED WITH PESSIMISM? Don't know about "tinged"...

3. DIFFICULTY IN DECISION MAKING? Not sure whether to answer that or not...

4. UNABLE TO THINK OF, OR DO, TWO THINGS AT ONCE?
I thought I had a cup of tea somewhere... I did make it, didn't I?

5. BLUNTING OF FEELING? APATHY, INDIFFERENCE?
Who *cares* about the tea? Who cares the world is getting hotter? I'll be gone soon.

6. RESISTANT TO CHANGE?
Who wants change? Things can only get worse.

7. LACK OF SPONTANEITY?
Yes, thank God. Lack of spontaneity has kept me out of all sorts of trouble.

8. GREATER CAUTION?
Definitely. It's being cautious that stops the life-threatening spontaneity.

9. INCREASED ANXIETY?
He who is not anxious has no imagination.*

10. DISTRUST OF THE UNFAMILIAR?
Well, of course. You don't know where they've been.

"People who are anxious and pessimistic are more likely to get dementia," it says. Hey ho! So that's one more thing to get anxious and pessimistic about.

Oh dear! Apathy is the only answer. I'll have a bath. With apathy.

A trade name! APATHY for your BATH! The new, relaxing balm for your bath – APATHETICALM!

* Briggs

Great art in Alnwick

RECENTLY, I CAME across the most amazing painting I have ever seen. Everything about it is astounding, even its size: it is 36 feet wide and 24 feet high! Furthermore, it contains more than forty life-size figures – full-length figures, details from head to toe. And these are not just invented; they are portraits of real people all major writers of the past hundred years: Charlotte Brontë, Salman Rushdie, Jane Austen, George Eliot, Virginia Woolf, Samuel Beckett,

T S Eliot and another thirty or so.

It is almost unbelievable. The heads are extremely lifelike and very alive; they look as if they are smiling and talking to one another; it is almost like a party. They are gathered on two balconies, one real, the other painted, amid dark green roof girders, some real, some painted. It is almost impossible to believe, yet there it is.

All this may mean little to anyone who has never tried to do realistic painting, let alone portraits. Portraiture is immensely difficult.

After my six years of painting in art schools, I did try portraiture, as it seemed to be the only way to make a living from Fine Art. I even got a picture of my mum into the Royal Society of Portrait Painters exhibition and sat back waiting for the commissions to roll in from the aristocracy. But of course, they did not roll at all, so it was back to Commercial Art again.

The idea of life-size portraiture is unthinkable. Life-size, you almost need to paint in the eyelashes. Walt Whitman in this picture has his beard painted with separate hairs, a red lower eyelid and broken finger nails. Edward Lear has on a three-piece suit with an elaborate check pattern which is meticulously painted – every fold in the cloth and every single button in detail. You can see the hairs in his beard, too.

Wilfred Owen is deep in conversation with John Keats, while above them Ted Hughes, holding a copy of *Ariel*, gazes into the distance. George Orwell is throwing a book at us; it is in mid-air over the shoulder of Ernest Hemingway, Mark Twain is arguing with Robert Louis Stevenson.

In my painting days, 36 inches by 24 inches was a good, typical size for a canvas, but 36 FEET by 24 FEET! It's insane. But it gets even more insane. This astounding piece of work is found in a second-hand bookshop! And the bookshop is not in Florence, Paris or London, but in a defunct railway station! In a place with an unpronounceable name: ALNWICK, pronounced AN- NICK, innit?

The painting took two years to do, and is the work of Peter Dodd, a renowned animator, who is not the world famous painter he deserves to be.

The work was commissioned by Mary and Stuart Manley, owners of Barter Books. Peter Dodd's father helped Peter throughout.

Simplify, simplify

THERE IS TOO much of everything, isn't there? Just think of those olden days when there was only one radio programme. Then, simply because there was a war going on they had to create a second programme for the Forces. So we had two, the Home Service and the Forces Programme, which later became the Home and the Light. Quite complicated enough, but then they created another high-brow one called the Third Programme. The rot had set in. How many are there now? Who knows? And that's without the television stations which I've just attempted to count. In the end, I had to give up, but it was over 90. Then, recently, a young kiddie of 44 was showing me his on-screen list of nine programmes and films he had recorded that week. When on earth will he find time to watch them, on top of all the new stuff coming in every day? There was a time when television didn't start till six. Now it's on 24 hours a day, plus "websites" where you can see yet more when each programme ends.

In the midst of writing this, the new *Oldie* arrived, and upon opening it, half a ton of leaflets splattered out all over the floor – clothes, books, gifts, charities, insurances, music, cards and posters.

Incredibly, in the midst of these concerns, I find I am thinking of getting one of these plastic electric pad things – I-pods? e-pads? I-books? R-soles? This has been almost forced upon me as my publisher, the renowned Jonathan Cape, is now publishing electric books. My editor, on the phone, hugely recommended one of them, a 'graphic novel' (strip cartoons, I call them) so I asked him to send me a list of the eBooks. Oh no, not possible, nothing on paper, the list is electric too. So, if I want to read these books, I've got to get an electric pad, pod gadget. Kandle! is that it?

Then, only last night I came across a quote from Thoreau's *Walden*: "our life is frittered away by detail... simplify, simplify." But will I? Will anyone? I've been reading wonderful, wise quotes from that book for the last half century, but never actually read it. Let's hope there is an electric *Walden*.

The Fear Index by Robert Harris is set in a hedge fund building which is entirely electric. Staff are fined for bringing in the slightest bit of paper. So there's an idea for you, Ingrams. What about an electric *Oldie*?

P.S. Ye gods! Blow me down. Having just started reading the magazine, I see our highly esteemed and pressed editor has done just that! You can now get The Oldie *by electricity. But why stop there? Why not make* The Oldie *HQ the UK's first paperless office?*

But don't forget you will also have to install the world's first all-electric lavatories!

The horror of
blood-red wombs

MY MOTHER, BORN in 1895
in a two-up two-down terrace
house with eleven other children
conceived and born in it, was told
nothing about menstruation. One
day she ran home from school,
sobbing in terror, with blood
running down her leg. She thought
she was dying.

Throughout my ten years of
primary and secondary schools,
there was not one word of sex
education. My parents also said

nothing. At grammar school, in
our first lesson with Mr Dennis,
the biology master, we were all
nudging one another in gleeful
anticipation: "This is the bloke...
he'll be the one who... you know...
worrgh!" But there was never a
single mention of IT. Not even in
the Fifth Form, where most of the
boys were fully developed and quite
capable of creating any number of
pregnancies. There was not even a
mention of animals doing IT, not

even the boring old birds and bees. We never got beyond single-cell life forms like the amoeba.

But, in the last year of primary school, my friend Terry Dooley brought a book that his parents had given him into the playground. One section had a series of pictures showing the developing baby in the womb. These were painted pictures, but done as if they were X-ray photographs, all in glorious Technicolor, mostly blood-red.

I was shocked. I couldn't believe what I was seeing. The baby was inside the mother! How could one human being be inside another? It must mean I had been inside my mother. Right inside her body, with her walking around with me inside. It was difficult to believe.

For a few moments, I was speechless, stunned. Then I managed to say feebly: "Yeah... oh yeah..." pretending I already knew. Terry and Pete Smith were laughing at me. I had probably gone pale and given the game away.

Later at home, the second shocking realisation dawned. If the baby was inside the mother, if I was inside my mother, how did it, how did I, get out?

Mercifully, I don't remember any pictures of spread thighs and splayed labia with a hairy head poking through. I don't think I could have borne that at the time. I probably would have fainted. Mum and me doing that? Me in there... right in between her... inside her... thing... whatever it was called...

Then, a mere couple of generations later, having given an eight-year-old girl a little leaping ballet dancer, supported on a wire rod, I said: "It's not very nice the way that wire goes through her pants and into her bottom." She replied: "It doesn't go into her bottom, it goes into her vagina where the babies come out." Also, walking along with two girls, one twelve and the other ten...

Twelve-year-old: "With this on my front, I look as if I'm pregnant."

Ten-year-old: "Well, if you are pregnant, it must be Jack Simmons'."

Twelve-year-old: "I can't be pregnant, I haven't started my periods yet, so it must be Jesus'."

It was inspiring to hear a young girl unconsciously brushing aside centuries of sexual repression and shame, together with religious myth, all in a single sentence.

The chick from the black stuff

GAZING OUT OF the kitchen window this morning, I saw two large patches of some black stuff beside the garden path. What could they possibly be? They certainly weren't there yesterday evening. Puzzled, I went out to take a closer look.

As I drew near, I saw they were feathers. Oh no! Not my Chicky! She had not come for breakfast this morning and I was getting worried, as she is very punctual and always

comes before eight. It was now half past. Lately, she has taken to sleeping out somewhere; her own poo-plastered shed has been abandoned. I have no idea where she goes at night. Perhaps she is a nympho chick? It's worrying but there's nothing to be done about it.

Were they my Chicky's feathers? I bent down and started sorting through them... yes, they were my Chicky's feathers all right – at first sight black, but the black is really a very dark green, with gold running up the spine and with a splash of white at the tip. My Chicky had gone. I would never see her again.

Living alone here, she has been a big part of my life for more than twelve months now. Something to care for, to think about, shop for, clear up after and worry about. Not quite as bad as having a child, let alone a baby, only a slight burden, and at that a pleasant one. Our border collie, Jess, died two years ago.

I gathered up the feathers and went into the kitchen to look through them. I wanted to keep one or two in memory of her. Sentimental tosh! I hear you cry... well, so be it, tosher. I then looked into her shed, at the pile of Jessie's old blankets where she often slept, the stack of poo-encrusted *Oldie* magazines at the other end of the shelf, Jessie's bed, on the edge of which she often perched and the dog's water bowl on which she often spent the night. The pram where she roosted under its hood. I'd not looked into it since she stopped laying long ago, having produced 41 eggs.

I went over to the pram and looked inside the hood – and, lo and behold there was an egg! Cold as stone, it had been lying on the baby's pillow for weeks, but together with the feathers, it would make a memorial for her.

At this very moment, as I write this, my dear Chicky is inside a fox, being digested, and soon she, the Champion Poo-Producer of all time, will be transposed into a poo herself.

Poor old Chicky. I do miss her. The many dedicated readers of my column will remember Chicky's arrival, how she came strutting in from heaven knows where, taking over the garden and then taking me over as well. Following me everywhere, sitting on my lap, pecking about on my shoulders, even getting into the car with me. She was such a nuisance.

Nudes, spivs and toffs

INSTEAD OF PLAYING a tape – sorry, disc thing – an oldie will sometimes re-run a childhood memory. It is less noisy and intrusive than a film and less fiddly to switch on. Furthermore, there are no American accents to decipher.

In 1947, my friend Mike's father was box office manager of the Globe Theatre in Shaftesbury Avenue. Mr Hinton could often get us free seats if a show was not booked up. We even got in to see the famous bare ladies at the Windmill Theatre, and saw the men scrambling over the seat backs to get nearer the front whenever someone left.

Mike and I were unimpressed by the bare ladies, perhaps because at thirteen we were too young. They seemed rather plump and pink, and although not wearing bras or pants, they were covered all over in a gauze mesh. The sort of stuff Mum put over meat to keep the flies off. Also, like meat, they never moved. It was not allowed by the Lord Chamberlain.

We much preferred Arthur English, the cockney spiv comedian of the day. He always wore a spiv's wide tie and, as he was telling his jokes, the tie grew longer and longer without him touching it. Down past his waist it went, past his knees, onto the stage and then dangled into the orchestra pit. Yards of it. We thought this was hilarious, much more exciting than the ladies, who were so bored they often chatted to one another on the stage.

One summer day we went to the Globe to collect some tickets and found Mike's father in his box office, talking to a very posh lady and two boys of about our age. She was obviously friendly with Mr Hinton and was talking to him about her boys. These two hovered there, beautifully dressed in crisp, white, short-sleeved shirts and pressed flannels – their perfectly tanned, public school arms graced with expensive watches. Mike and I waited nervously just behind them. Then Mr Hinton pointed past the lady and the boys and said, "That's my boy, there." These three creatures from another planet turned and looked at us for a long moment, and said nothing. Then the lady turned back to Mr Hinton and murmured something polite.

The lady turned out to be Mrs Emlyn Williams.

P.S. for juveniles who have never heard of Emlyn Williams, look him up on Guggle – or whatever it's called.

Stollidges and all that

ONE OF THE few good things about old age is that you still have a foothold in another world – the world of your youth. This is now so far away and so extraordinary that younger people can scarcely believe it ever existed, particularly if it happened in a place they now know well.

My neighbour Tom, a retired farmer soon to be ninety years old, has lived here all his life. He was born in our local pub, in 1925, one of nine brothers and sisters. His father ran the pub part-time as he was mainly a farmer. The beer was in wooden barrels with wooden

taps; and these stood on low wooden stools, which Tom says were called "stollidges". (Can't find it in the OED, so possibly a dialect word?) two or three made the taps difficult to get at, as they were at knee level. His father got fed up with this, so he bought a garden watering can, filled it from a barrel and used it to pour the beer into the glasses.

Today, it is a smart "gastro-pub" with candlelit tables, menus and wine lists. Wine is in old-fashioned glass bottles with not a watering can in sight.

There was no electricity, no gas, and no running water, let alone hot water. Outside was a well, with the usual lever pump and a bucket. Lighting was by oil lamps. There was no heating apart from the coal-fired kitchen range and open fires.

Tom's mother did not buy her flour in paper bags from shops; she bought it in quarter-hundred weight sacks.

There was no heating at all in the bedrooms, but as the children slept three to a bed, they all survived. Baths were taken in a tin bath which was kept outside hanging on the wall, so there was no need for a "bathroom". The lavatory was at the far end of the "garden", and you usually had to find your way to it through some peacefully grazing cows.

Today, it is a paved garden terrace with flowering shrubs, dining tables and waitresses flitting about.

In the front of the pub was a flint wall with rings set in it. This was where any passing cavalry, dropping in for a pint, would tether their horses.

Horses were an essential part of farming at that time. Tom's father, farming since 1921, only got his first tractor in 1938. Before then, everything was done by horses. The four in the picture were called Traveller, Jack, Prince and Darling, and they still had two horses working in 1953.

Beer was fourpence a pint (old pence, yoof – 240 to the pound) and ten fags were fourpence. One old boy used to come in regularly, put a tanner down on the bar, get his ten fags for fourpence and half a pint of beer for tuppence.

Obviously, there was no telly, no phones, no mobiles, no computers, no internet and no car. However, they did get a wireless set in the mid-thirties. This was powered by a huge, glass, acid-filled battery, and once a week a man came up from a shop in the village to take the empty battery away to charge it. This cost fourpence. As no one else had a wireless, neighbours would crowd in on Christmas day to hear the King's speech.

P.S. We have a Czech person staying with us at the moment. She says they have "stollidges" in her language – small, heavy, wooden stools. But being foreign, they spell it wrong: STOLICKY.

Even so, it's better than the OED, who can't spell it at all.

CUTTING-EDGE STATION STOPS

HAMPSHIRE – FOR QUALITY OF LIFE says the road sign on the border. Quality? What quality? Good quality? Poor quality? "Never mind the quality – feel the width" of Hampshire. Are there no unemployed in Hampshire, no drugs, no crime?

HAYWARDS HEATH ♥ OF MID SUSSEX. If that place is the heart, Heaven help the rest of Sussex.

Who writes this garbage? More importantly, why?

A battered old builder's lorry proclaims on its side: SUPPLYING THE CUTTING EDGE. The cutting edge of what? Bricks? Sand and cement?

CONSIGNIA. Our dearly beloved 200-year-old Royal Mail nearly got changed to Consignia. It cost a million or two, but mercifully, never came to be. No one could spell it, few could pronounce it. Besides, it is a derogatory word – consigned to prison, consigned to the rubbish dump.

"The SERVICE standing at Platform 4 –". A "service" can't stand anywhere. It's a train, for God's sake. And we are not "customers", we are passengers. Also, "The next STATION STOP" is a station. That's what stations are for, isn't it? It's where the trains stop. Don't they know that?

THANK YOU FOR TRAVELLING WITH SOUTHERN. What the hell else are we going to do? Walk the 50 miles from Brighton? Hire a helicopter? Hop on a bus for two or three hours?

And those vans in London – RUNNING WATER FOR YOU (So clever! The copywriter must have dined out on that one.) Down here they are not running water for us, they are running it for the Australians. Our South East Water was bought by the Frogs who then flogged it to the Aussies.

RUNNING WATER FOR AUSSIE SHAREHOLDERS. They don't put that on the vans. No wonder we've had a drought. They've got deserts out there, haven't they?

Bring back creative sociopaths

HAVING RECENTLY WRITTEN of my discovery that I am a stereotype, it was a relief to find that the label does have its compensations.

Also, for the last 17 years, I have had on the wall of my workroom an article from *The Times* by the great Doctor Stuttaford. It has stood me in good stead for almost two decades. Thanks a million, doc!

"Why gifted artists Pay a High Price for their vocation", is the title. "Creative people often find it difficult to comply with the demands of a prosaic world. The artistically gifted are frequently so dedicated to their vocation, whether it is music, visual arts or writing, that they can appear SELF-ABSORBED, IMPULSIVE, IMPATIENT and INTOLERANT. [yes! *My CAPS*. R.B.] Even in my medical lifetime there was a sub-group whom psychiatrists labelled creative sociopaths – a term now abandoned."

What a shame! I like it. I am definitely a creative sociopath. I am impatient and intolerant of stupid PC people wanting to tidy up the language. What's wrong with being self-absorbed? It's better than being absorbed in someone else, so "in love" that you can't think straight or get on with work. Also, it's being impulsive and impatient that gets things done, otherwise you might spend hours gawping at your mobile phone or garbage on the telly. In the War, it was intolerance that got rid of Hitler, Buchenwald and Belsen.

Being labelled a psychiatric type with a proper title is reassuring. It helps you to understand who you are and where you stand. It gives you the kind of reassurance that religions must give their believers. "You are a sinner!" Er... well, yes, I suppose so. "You will burn in Hell!" Um... oh dear. I'd better try and be good then.

Millions of people find this comforting. At least it tells them what they are and where they are going. So why should we creative sociopaths be denied the comfort of our label?

We won't go to Hell, will we?

All our yesterdays

EVERYONE KNOWS THAT the older you get, the faster time goes. Nevertheless, every so often something crops up which gives you a shock.

The other day, I picked up a shiny, new booklet which has been lying around in my work room for ages: Penguin Author Guide. It is just a routine list of the departments: Editorial, Marketing, Royalties, Exports, etc. All pretty routine and slightly boring, but you are supposed to know about it. If someone had asked me how long I had had the booklet, I would have said: 'Oh, months... maybe almost a year... Still, allowing for Old Age always underestimating the passing of time... I'd better say a year and a bit.' I'd hardly looked at it so, duty-bound, I picked it up and opened it. The first thing I noticed was that against every head of department's name was a large fax number. Fax! What's that? I did remember it, just, as my own fax thing is still in a corner of the room. Quite a few insects seem to live in it and they come out now and again for a breath of air. A large brown spider lives in there, too. Just as I was puzzling over this fax business, a neatly folded, crisp, new-looking letter fell out of the booklet. When I picked it up, I saw it was from Nicola, a commissioning editor I'd always had a friendly, jokey relationship with. She had hand-written a note at the bottom of the letter saying: "I'll be phoning soon to check that you have read this properly." Like most office girlies, Nicola left some time ago to have babies and get married. Then I saw the date on the letter: 16 March 2000! TWELVE YEARS AGO! I still cannot believe it.

These last twelve years seem to have passed by without a thought – just trolling along as usual, fiddling about, writing occasional bits of tripe, nothing much to report: half a dozen deaths of course, but that's life. Compare it with another twelve-year period, say 1939, when I was five, to 1951, when I was seventeen. There were a few things to remember there: the little matter of a World War for a start. Roof blown off our house, every window shattered, evacuation, return home to doodle bugs overhead, explosions; starting at so-called grammar school 1944, art school 1949 (painting naked ladies), first motorbike, then going to the Festival of Britain with my first girlfriend in 1951.

Phew! It makes me tired just to write it, let alone live it. I'm glad I'm old now and peacefully half-asleep... fax machines... motorbikes... girlfriends... zzzz...

All tied up

THE ABSURDITY OF dress codes: where do they come from? Fashion may decree, but in the end, class dictates.

The oddest item has been the tie. Back in the fifties, it was obligatory. Going to the doctor, dentist, bank manager – put a tie on, though the chances were, you were wearing one already. Recently, I came across a self-portrait I painted at that time – sat in our kitchen at home and wearing a jacket and tie. A teenage art student!

At grammar school, we were forbidden to travel home in part-uniform. So even on the hottest day we were expected to cycle several miles wearing a thick black blazer, a cap and a tie. I used to dive into an alleyway, take off all three bits and bung them into my saddlebag.

Then later, came the restaurant nonsense. Some posh places insisted that customers wore a tie. If you turned up tieless, they would lend you one. Gad! Improperly dressed, what? I only suffered that humiliation once, and, of course, never went there again.

Much worse than that was the well-known story of the glamorous young woman who was asked to leave a restaurant she had just entered, because she was wearing trousers. Fortunately, she had on a trouser suit, so she marched into the Ladies, whipped off the trousers and came out with the tunic top just about long enough to pass as a mini-skirt. Apparently, that was quite acceptable. I bet it was.

But this kind of nonsense becomes ingrained. Even now, despite being an habitual sandal-wearer, I feel I cannot go to a doctor, hospital or dentist in sandals.

Consequently, I was almost shocked to see a bloke waiting in our dentist's reception wearing a stained and filthy vest. Not a T-shirt, but an underwear vest, hairy armpits and all, and apart from his skull, unshaven as well. Gad! I thought, the fellow isn't even wearing a tie.

All this piffle began for me in the early fifties. In my transition from working class to middle class I found there was a lot to learn.

One afternoon, my girlfriend and I came back to her house and her mother asked me to stay to "supper". We called it "tea" at home. Supper was something you had just before going to bed, if you were feeling peckish. Cornflakes, usually.

It was a hot summer day, so I was wearing an open-neck shirt and the usual gabardine raincoat. When I took the raincoat off, the mother's face fell.

"Haven't you got a jacket?"

"Oh... er – no."

"You must have a jacket.'

"Oh, no... I'm fine, thanks. Not cold at all."

"Julian, darling, get him a jacket."

My girlfriend's brother led me up to his room and I put on one of his jackets and a tie. The jacket was far too big as he was a public school rugger type and I was a suburban weed. I went downstairs swamped by this green tweed jacket, with the sleeves down to my knuckles and the shoulders drooping off me.

Throughout the meal, the brother and I sat sweltering in these jackets and ties, while the women wore summer blouses with low necks and bare arms. It was not a formal occasion, only the four of us.

I thought, if this is how the middle class lives, then bollocks to it.

Old age adage

ALMOST ALL OLDIES know the old adage: "Three things happen in old age:

1. You lose interest in sex;
2. Your family drifts apart;
3. You lose touch with old friends.

And these are just the three main advantages."

However cynical this may sound, all are true. Number One does provide relief, particularly if there had been any wickedness "on the side". The lies, the deception, the alibis... all very tiresome, I should think. Don't know how people manage it. Perhaps, I should give it a try

before it's too late..? Oh yes, sorry, it *is* too late; I forgot.

Family drifts apart? Well, that's inevitable. A friend of mine, same age as I am, has five sons and daughters, now in their forties, all living in distant parts of the world. This is a mixed blessing, as with increasing old age, you will often need them. "Hi, Luke, it's Dad. I need a bit of help getting to the bathroom at night... sorry to bother you... I know Zimbabwe is quite a way off, but any chance of you popping over?"

Luckily, I have no descendants to call on, so I will have to soldier bravely on alone. Being lifelong self-employed should be a help, of course.

Number three is the worst, but it does happen. For years I've been trying to think why. Lack of energy must be the main cause. Go down the pub in the late evening? Er... no thanks, not now... bit tired, was going to have an early night. Drive twelve miles to meet for a coffee? Well, another day perhaps? Hope to see you soon... sorry I've been out of touch but things are a bit difficult here at the moment... I'll give you a ring... next week, perhaps... when I get the chance.

But do not despair! Another bunch of chums will soon come rolling in to keep you company. All with funny names. Dear old CREEKY NEES, American by the sound of him, then there's A. KINBAK, most oldies know him well. CHILL BLANES calls regularly. Odd names they've all got. ARTHUR RITUS and RUE MATTIZUM, French possibly, are both fairly regular visitors. But then comes the heavy mob: PA KINSONS stays a long time – gets you jumping about, or makes you sit nice and still – then there's AL ZEIMERS and his pal D. MENSHER. And, of course, there's always dear old D. PRESHUN, who will frequently be dropping in for a chat about "life".

Oh ho! What a cheery note to end on. But never mind, Christmas is coming!

Oh, no it isn't, sorry. It's been and gone. But I've just had a more profound thought:

SELF DOUBT
They say that
in old age
you lose touch
with old friends.

But maybe,
in old age
it is old friends
who lose touch
with you?

Now, that's a bit more cheery, isn't it?

The Excreman

THE STRANGEST BOOK I've ever seen arrived recently. It had been sent from Hong Kong and was called *The Excreman*. The publisher who sent it said it had been inspired by my book *The Snowman*.

The Snowman, naturally, is made of snow and the Excreman is made of... well, you can guess. The story opens with a view of the exterior of a building at night. The next pictures move into a close-up of mother and child and we see that they are pink pigs. The mother wears a mauve dress, but the pig child is naked except for a Father Christmas hat which he wears throughout the story. He then goes to the lavatory, squats on it, looking dissatisfied. The following two frames show a brown abstract chaos of crisp packets, sweet wrappers and all the stuff he has been eating swirling along in the gloom. The last frame shows him grinning with satisfaction.

Then, as he is about to pull the chain he sees a small brown poo figure come floating to the surface. He is a cheery little chap with a friendly smile, pink and green Smarties for eyes and a green leaf for a nose. Our pink pig hero closes the lid on him with some reluctance, then goes to bed, still in his Father Christmas hat.

In the middle of the night, a huge brown figure comes quietly into the bedroom. The poo man has come out of the lavatory and grown enormously. At first the little pink pig is terrified, but then the giant poo man starts looking at three photographs on the bedroom wall. These show our pink pig as a small baby wearing a pretty white bonnet and squatting on a chamber pot. The other two pictures show his mother proudly tipping the chamber pot slightly, so we can admire the tiny poos in it.

Piggy and Pooman become friends, and as in *The Snowman*, Piggy makes Pooman a scarf. He pulls yards of pink toilet paper from the roll and wraps it round Pooman's neck. Then a chamber pot upside down makes a perfect hat for Pooman. When the hat is on, Pooman takes Piggy's hand and they fly round the room, swooping down to the lavatory then plunging into the bowl and descending into the dark, endless immensity of Pooland. Here they eventually arrive in a vast space lined with huge metal pipes, and encounter a poo-man rock band. A singer, three guitars and drums are all hard at it, in front of an audience of poo-people.

There is much more... a music score, is printed and a film is in production. The story is by Brian Tse and Alice Mak.

There is merchandise, too. With the book came an Excreman soft toy, which about ten inches high, and sits with his legs stretched out in front of him, and wears a white woolly chamber pot on his head. When you squeeze his left hand he sings you a song in a charming Oriental accent, his legs beating up and down in time to the music.

"Hollo, hollo, how are yo? Hollo, hollo, hollo, how are yo? Thank yo, thank yo, I am fine. And I hope that yo are too." You can't stop him until he has finished.

It is impossible to comment on such an extraordinary work. The book is wordless and it leaves any would-be commentator wordless too.

Let's talk rude

REMEMBERING THOSE RUDE words of childhood, and how they changed as we grew older. For instance, in my time, the word "penis" was never used. In primary school and at home, the word was "johnny". I doubt if my mother had ever heard of "penis". Later, at secondary school, it was "dick"; "johnny" was for babies. Then, grown up and in the army, it became "cock". In recent years, dealing with grandchildren, we all say "willy". Though now, as they are nearing teens, they no longer find it bearable, let alone funny. Recently, I made a feeble joke about willies and the 12-year-old closed her eyes, shook her head slowly and said wearily: "Oh, Raymond..."

One of the most unmentionable words of my childhood was "spunk". This seems to have died out; it is decades since I heard it used. I can remember once bringing home my copy of the *Dandy*, opening it and there in bold letters right across the page was the title of a new series: THE FIVE SPUNKY

DUNCANS. I could not believe what I was seeing. I was shocked and embarrassed. I even tried to hide the comic from my mother as if it were pornography, though probably she would never have heard of the word, let alone have known what spunk was.

I think the *Dandy* came from Dundee, so that may explain it. Those Scots!

But prudery still lingers on in some oldie minds. Back in the eighties, I did a cartoon for the *Guardian*, using the very words I had heard a 12-year-old girl use to explain sexual intercourse to her 10-year-old brother. (He knew already, but being rather absent-minded, had forgotten.)

"You must know *that*! The man's penis gets stiff, he puts it into the woman's vagina, the sperm comes out, goes into the womb and fertilises the egg cell. Everybody knows that."

"Oh yeah... yeah... we did it at school. I forgot... any more Frosties?"

The then editor was shocked by this text and phoned me with a suggestion.

"Couldn't we just say the man puts his thingummy in the woman's wotsit?"

I couldn't believe what I was hearing. Was this really the *Guardian* in the Eighties? It felt more like the *Lady* magazine of the Fifties. The expurgated cartoon was published, but the joke had been destroyed and the whole point was lost.

"Expurgated" sounds quite rude, doesn't it? "George was expurgated by Mike", or even worse, "George was bowdlerised by Mike."

Old phallus

SIR: Sylvia J Elliott is mistaken in thinking my article was "about the male member". It was about language and how it changes over time. "Male member" itself is a good example of linguistic change. Today, only an oldie would use it.

Everyone else would think it was a bloke in the House of Commons.

Raymond Briggs, via email

Worlds apart

IT IS SURPRISING how we all get on with one another despite each of us living in our own separate world.

Recently, I phoned a cousin to tell her about a programme I knew she would be sorry to miss. Despite being in her seventies (poor old thing) she is of sound mind. Yes, Daphne, I said, it's next Tuesday, eight o'clock, Radio 4. Just a minute, she said – get a pencil. (No pencil by the phone! Perhaps she is not of sound mind after all.) Right, she said. Tuesday, eight o'clock, Channel 4.

No! I screeched, not *Channel 4*, *Radio 4*!

Stunned silence.

Oh... she said, in a wondering voice.

Radio 4... I'll see if I can find it then...

How can a sensible woman, born in this country before the War, Home Service, Alvar Lidell etc., never have heard of Radio 4? OK, she didn't listen to it, but...

What world is she living in? What world am I living in?

It brought back a memory of a

few decades ago. A friend's wife mentioned someone called Tony Bennett. Oh, I said, who's he? The lady gaped at me, speechless. It was like the ham acting in a silent film. She sank onto the sofa, still wordless and staring at me as if I was an alien.

Embarrassed, I said, I *do* know *Arnold* Bennett. But I don't think she had heard of him.

Then recently, while a friend and I were visiting her daughter, we were sitting around chatting when, suddenly, all the electrics went off.

Immediately, I sprang to my feet, and as the only alpha-male present, took control of the emergency. The trip, I barked, where's the trip? Trip? came the bewildered reply. Yes! The trip! It's in the fuse box. Where is it? Fuse box? she said.

This woman – mid-thirties, ex-university, successful business career – not only did she not know where her own fuse box was, she had never heard of such a thing. How had she survived eighteen years without mummy and daddy? What world is she living in? Mind you, she only did an arts degree – literature or something. So perhaps that explains it.

It reminded me of one day, back in the fifties, when I discovered that my first-ever girlfriend had never heard of Frank Sinatra. Even in those days, it was beyond belief. I can't remember now what I said. Stunned silence, probably.

No wonder we never got married.

IT'S THE PROM

YESTERDAY, A MAGNIFICENT open landau swept past my window; top-hatted coachman, gleaming black coach, cream leather seats, and a pair of glossy black horses with white plumes on their heads... in seconds they were gone.

What could this be? A couple of minor royals being met at the station? Coming down to view my work perhaps? I dashed across the road to Mary, our neighbour, who knows everything, to see if I needed to put a tie on.

Mary! Did you see that landau? Where on earth is it going?

Oh, it's the prom, she said.

Prom? I said. What – the Albert Hall?

No, said Mary, laughing. The school.

School? I was baffled.

It turned out that, at the end of the summer term, the 16-year-old children celebrate "leaving school". Of course, it's all pretend. They haven't left at all; they've barely started on the education treadmill. They still have two years of

sixth form to get through and then three years of so-called "uni". So what is there to celebrate?

Incredibly, the boy children dress up like Daddy in black tie, and the little girls doll themselves up in what must be their granny's wedding frock from the fifties, all petticoats and froth. (I've now seen the photographs.)

Children from the council estate packed into a white stretch-limo to be driven a couple of miles to the reception, in a pub! They were accompanied by a fleet of vintage cars, pre-war Daimlers, Bentleys and American Fifties automobiles with enormous fins.

Has our world gone mad? We're supposed to be in an economic crisis, aren't we? No money for "Education, education, education". It's just cuts, cuts, cuts...

Someone said this "proms" piffle was just copying America. It must be true; the sheer awfulness bears it out. Any more education cuts and we'll end up with a Bush-moron as Prime Minister.

The food of love?

NOTHING SEPARATES US more by age than our choice of music. Reading in the paper today a list of groups, bands... whatever they are called nowadays, I feel that once again I do not belong; it is another world. But fortunately, it was part of a people-matching scheme used by a dating agency, and I certainly don't belong there. My dating days are done, thank heaven. Nevertheless, if you come across any sizzling swingers in their seventies, do let me know!

Most of the names on this list I have never heard of, let alone heard their music. So, test yourself now! Pencil and paper at the ready. 1 Adele? No. 2 Kings of Leon? No. 3 Arctic Monkeys? Yes! Heard the name but only because Gordon Brown claimed to be a fan. Probably they were Scottish. 4 Arcade Fire? No. 5 Muse? No. 6 Radiohead? Vaguely heard name. 7 Lady Gaga? Heard of, seen rude pictures in gutter press, as I was passing by. 8 Foo Fighters? No. 9 Coldplay? Heard name.

10 Rihanna? No. 11 Daft Punk? No. 12 Kanye West? No. 13 Nirvana? No. 14 Katy perry? No. 15 the Beatles? Yes; have two Long playing Gramophone Recordings! 'LPs', 33 RPMm (Revolutions per minute), 12 inches wide, on Vinyl! Just get that, yoof! Cool? 16 Red Hot Chili Peppers? No. 17 Pink Floyd? Heard of, quite famous. 18 Eminem? No. 19 Linkin Park? No. 20 Metallica? No.

So, how did you rate? What kind of partner will you get? Will he or, she, be hot stuff?

For consolation, I turned to the *Radio Times* and tonight there are the King's Singers. I have heard of them and heard their music, all very respectable, but found I did not belong with their list either. Most of the names I had never heard of and had not heard the music either. So here we go again: 1 Bennett? (Not Alan, not Arnold, certainly not Tony) no. 2 Weelkes? No. 3 Ligeti? Heard of. 4 Bartlett? No. 5 Gibbons? No (not Caroll, I shouldn't think). 6 Ravenscroft? No. 7 Wilbye? no, 8 Williamson? No. 9 Elena Kats-Chernin? No, but she sounds as if she should be on the other list. With a name like that she could hardly fail. "This week, pop-pickers, at number one we have Kats-Chernin!" As Jane Austen said somewhere: "One half of the world cannot understand the pleasures of the other."

So this music test, called a Love Chart, is a very good way of sorting people out. It would certainly sort out any wicked old men on the prowl. Or, for that matter, any wicked old women.

Phew!

2013: THE SIXTIETH ANNIVERSARY of the end of the Korean war.

"ALREADY?" I hear fellow oldies gasp in disbelief. "SIXTY YEARS!"

"Korean war?'" says a young kiddy in his fifties. "What's that? A war? When? Korea...?"

Eighteen-year-old British National Servicemen, boys just out of school, were killed there. By a lucky fluke of timing, I just missed it. As an art student on a four-year course, I had been given

a deferment of one year from National Service. The war was still going on in 1952 when I became 18. My course was due to end in 1953 and I prayed that this stupid war would end by then. Risk my life to save South Korea from going communist? No, thank you. Over half the world was communist already, so what difference would this little bit make? A small peninsula, thousands of miles away on the other side of the world, the northern half of which was already communist? Who cares tuppence if the southern half goes communist, too? At least it would be tidier. Would you lay down your life to stop it? Luckily, it did end in 1953. Phew! Just missed it.

My father was even luckier. Recently, I wrote a bit about his skilful good fortune:

MY DAD AND THE HISTORY OF THE TWENTIETH CENTURY
Even before he was born,
My dad,
Swimming about in the waters,
Knew exactly when to get out.

Born,
5 November 1900.

Fourteen,
5 November 1914. Too young.

Eighteen,
5 November 1918. Just ripe for slaughter.

Six days later,
11 November 1918, war ends.

Armistice
Phew!
Just missed it.

1939,
here we go again.
Thirty-nine now, too old.

Phew!
Just missed it again.

Well done, Dad.
you deserve a medal,
For Life Saving.

———————————————

Obes, obesses and obies

"BARBARA CASTLE'S ROUND the corner. Get the gun out and shoot the bugger." This was said to me in a strong Sussex accent by an old farm worker, pointing at the glass in my hand. I was standing by the door of our local, the Half Moon, and he was only half joking.

The new drink-driving laws had just been introduced and the whole pub was fuming. How dare they interfere with our freedom to drink as much as we liked then drive home? What could be more natural? Been doing it for years. Our three dedicated alcoholics were always

there, running back and forth twice a day in their Morris Minors. They are all long since dead.

It now seems incredible that we thought this was perfectly all right. I can also remember driving home from parties, on icy roads in the depths of winter, saying to myself: Now, keep your eyes on the centre line, cling on to that and keep slow and steady... then when I at last got home, feeling a sense of satisfaction that I had accomplished a very difficult task successfully.

Unbelievable. No thought that I might have injured a child, put a young woman into a wheelchair for the rest of her life, or even killed someone. All for the sake of a few glasses of wine.

What are we doing today that in twenty years time we will look back upon with disbelief, even disgust?

The most likely candidate for this must surely be obesity. It probably kills more people than alcohol and now is almost an epidemic. Millions are being spent on building bigger morgues capable of taking corpses weighing up to 50 stone. I should have thought anyone weighing 50 stone would be delighted to be dead. Every week, when we go into the town, we relieve the boredom of shopping by counting the number of obes and obesses we see. Outside the bakery are public benches and these are always occupied by two or three obesses with their buggies filled with their obies. They are all stuffing themselves from paper packets held in their hands – the mums leaning forward, still chomping, to stuff the little obies. This is at about 11 in the morning, so what meal is that? A late breakfast, or an early lunch? Do they know, or care? Perhaps they just chomp away all day like animals in a field.

Someone in the future may say: "What! You allowed people to gobble junk food as much as they liked, even though it was causing diabetes, heart disease and even death? Furthermore, and more importantly, it was costing the National Health Service millions of pounds every year."

What can be done? High taxes on unhealthy foods? Doctors refusing to treat obes who will not try to lose weight? It all sounds like the nanny state or even fascism, but it is surely better than a slow death for thousands of people?

Nanny state is what many people thought when the anti-smoking laws came in, but now smokers must go outdoors and the fag packets have SMOKING KILLS on them. What can we put on the fast food packets? Or perhaps we should just get the gun out? But who to shoot?

Obes, obesses, obies

SIR: My language is enriched. I am very grateful to Mr Briggs.

Frank Cowell, London

The back of the drawer

"KING'S LETTER ENCLOSED BELOW"

This was printed in caps on a bit of plain card framed by another layer of the same card.

Searching for something, I had opened a small drawer which I had not touched for many years. King? I thought: Dave King? Michael King? I had come across quite a few Kings since those two in primary school. But, why the frame? Why the formal printing?

Underneath it was another bit of paper about 7 by 5 inches: Royal Coat of Arms and BUCKINGHAM PALACE in red at the top. No address! Let alone a postcode. Also, why not His Majesty the King?

I greatly regret that I am unable to give you personally the award which you have so well earned.

I now send it to you with my congratulations and my best wishes for your future happiness.

GEORGE R.I.

6149094 Cpl. G. A. Barron, M.M., The East Surrey Regiment.

Under this was a very small cardboard box labelled

M.M.
6149094
CPL. G.A. BARRON
E. SURR. R.
15.6.43

Inside was the medal itself:

M.M. The Military Medal, won by my father-in-law. I had completely forgotten about it.

Then another yellowing bit of paper fell out; the Royal Coat of Arms embossed at the top, but with no colour; type-written in pale blue, probably a carbon copy. "Corporal BARRON took over command of a platoon when his Platoon Sergeant was wounded, and led it with great dash. Whilst on the Djebel Ang, on 14th April 1943, he was in the forward platoon which was heavily attacked, mortared and machine-gunned by the enemy. He kept his platoon intact under this heavy fire and repelled every frontal attack, while the Coy worked round the flanks. He retained his position under heavy fire until he was ordered to withdraw by his Coy Comd owing to heavy casualties. His leadership in the difficult task of Platoon Commander was exemplary."

Ye Gods! Dear old Gordon doing that! This quiet, self-effacing man was not remotely a scrum-half type yelling at his team for victory; quite the opposite.

Then there was another box:

dark green with three Royal Coats of Arms in gold on the lid. SPINK & SON LTD. KING STREET. ST JAMES LONDON. This contained six more medals: For Bravery in the Field, The 1939–1945 Star, The Africa Star 1st Army, The Italy Star, The Defence Medal, and the 1939–45 Medal.

I won the Kate Greenaway Medal twice, for illustrating kiddies' picture books, but it's not quite in the same league.

What should I do with these things? It's unthinkable to throw them away, but as I had forgotten them for thirty years, they might as well have been in the bin. Gordon and I were not all that close, though we liked one another well enough; he was not my father and when I am gone these will mean nothing to my descendants, as I haven't got any. People probably collect this kind of thing so, should I try and sell them and ask for the cheque to be made out to the British Legion? There must be hundreds, possibly thousands of people with things like these, forgotten in the backs of drawers. What should we do? Any advice, please?

P.S. When he was demobbed Gordon went back to his pre-war job as a travelling salesman for a clothing wholesaler. He used to take rackfuls of clothes all over East Anglia by train! Now that definitely deserves a medal.

Ireland is a very odd place

ONE DAY WHEN driving from Cork to Dingle, we stopped at a pub for lunch. In the gents, there was only one cubicle and its door had a peculiar hole cut in it. Anyone inside lost all privacy below the knees. Later, when I opened the door it struck against the lid of the pedestal which was to the right. I had to reach round and raise the lid. The door would then pass over the pedestal.

Obviously, someone had hung the door, opened it and found it struck the pedestal and blocked anyone trying to get in. So, instead of rehanging the door on the left, (too much trouble), he carved a pedestal shape out of the door. But even then, he must have cut the shape with the lid up. With the lid down, the door still struck against the lid and so would not open.

Then, in our hotel room in Cork, there was another peculiar door. The knob on the inside was not near the opening edge, as is the custom in the rest of the world, but was in the centre of the door and so almost useless. Furthermore, the door opened outwards into the corridor; not very convenient if someone was passing by with a trayload of china.

When we arrived, we found the carpet was so filthy we had to ask them to hoover it. Yet these same people changed the sheets every single day. Then, when I tried to wash, there was no plug in the basin. I phoned the desk and they brought one up and gave it to me. It didn't fit, so I had to phone them again. Why on earth was it not chained on as they are in the rest of the world?

On the outside of our door was the number 37 – the room next door was number 49. We were on the top floor, with nothing overlooking us except sky, yet out of the four panes in our sash window, three were of frosted glass, each with a different pattern.

Another time, staying with a friend in Dublin, I went into the lavatory on the landing of the large terrace house. It was already a hot summer day but the heat in this small windowless lavatory was unbearable. It was so hot I had to leave the door open to avoid suffocation. When I flushed the lavatory, I was enveloped in clouds of steam as gallons of very hot water gushed into the bowl.

If a writer had made up these incidents and put them in a comic Irish novel, they would be accused of caricature. But what is surprising is that these surreal happenings could be tolerated by the customer. Didn't the landlord of the pub complain to the carpenter? Hadn't the pub customers complained? Why did the hotel door open outwards? The expense of the hot-water lavatory would have had most people reaching for the phone, or a shotgun, the moment it was discovered.

But although Ireland is an odd place, it does have its compensations. Once when I arrived in Dublin, the lady meeting me had asked me to wait on a certain traffic island near the station, and she would come by and pick me up. I had only been on the island a few minutes when a middle-aged man came over to me, held out his arms and gently took my elbows. It was almost an embrace. "Are y' all right, my friend?" he said.

You could stand on a traffic island in Paris until you were a heap of whitened bones and nobody would give a damn.

Big bags and babies

WHEN WE WERE nine and ten-year-old kids, towards the end of the War, we were haunted by two horrible images. And despite the bomb sites all around, neither of them came from the War.

A small, dark-haired girl in our class at school said she had found her father's sperm on the lavatory seat and had put it into herself with her finger. Then, later, she had given birth to half a baby.

We were stunned by this and baffled. Was it possible? Why would she lie about it? We had never received a word of sex education, so we had no idea of what was possible and what was not.

Giving birth was fantastic enough, but half a baby?! The question then arose – which half? To give birth to a child with no hips and no legs was dreadful enough, but a child with legs and feet but with nothing above the waist – no arms, no head, no face, no voice... this was the essence of nightmare.

From then on, I felt quite fearful of this girl and kept away from her.

Whether it was true or not, it still meant she was a creepy person. If she had not actually done it, pretending that she had was almost as bad. What would she do or say next? She could easily tell fantastic lies about one of us. Even then, I must have had an instinct about avoiding paternity suits, despite never having heard of them.

About the same time, we were intrigued by a middle-aged, respectable couple in the park. Sex and babies again. We used to play football near the entrance to the now abandoned underground air-raid shelters, and this couple, both well-dressed in long coats and wearing hats, would regularly come past us and go down into the shelters.

We had often explored these long, dank, pitch-dark tunnels, with rough planks for seats on either side. There was no lighting, the floor was wet, the roof dripping. It was a depressing and frightening place.

The man always carried a very large black leather bag, smaller than a cricket bag, but much bigger than a doctor's bag.

What on earth were they doing down there? Why did they come so often? What was in the bag?

We immediately thought sex. Sex and Babies. We knew sex caused babies, but hadn't quite grasped the fact that you can do sex without babies. Did you need equipment to DO IT? Is that what was in the bag? Or were the babies in the bag? Or at least one baby? Why was the bag so big?

Even today, over half a century later, I would still like to know.

HOMO DUMBO

HOMO Sapiens? Homo Dumbo, more like. The time it took for us, the Dumbos, to think of the blindingly obvious.

When they eventually moved out of the caves and into the mud huts, the Dumbos lit fires in the middle of the lounge and nearly choked when the hut filled with smoke. Then a genius was born who invented The Hole in the Roof.

Untold centuries later, another genius invented The Chimney. What vision! However, the fire still smoked, so they made the mistake of trying to catch the smoke by making the chimney wider and wider, thus creating the idiotic inglenook fireplace, so beloved by Dumbo estate agents today.

It was not until the 19th century that Rumford came along and invented the narrow flue. This sucked out the smoke and the fire burned brighter and hotter. Decades later, it dawned on the Dumbos that half the heat was also sucked up the chimney and a stove was far better.

It is a similar story with the train. Early trains were a series of stage coaches set upon flat bed trucks. This pattern of carriage design persisted into the 1950s and 1960s! Four or five seats facing one another with a hinged door on either side. Madness. People fell out. Or, at a station in the dark, got out the wrong side and fell onto the track.

Also, once you were sitting in one of these and the train started moving, you were trapped inside with whoever happened to be there. Anything could happen and often did.

Then, another genius invented The Corridor. People could walk up and down the train inside it!

Many years later, a visionary must have cried aloud: "Why don't we have the corridor down the middle? Why have separate compartments at all? Save weight, save space, pack in more people."

Other Dumbo-isms persisted into recent times. We have a family joke about my father-in-law who was regularly summoned into his wife's bedroom to smooth out her rucked-up bottom sheet. For years on end, the poor man was made to turn out of his bed two or three times a week. He died young.

Then some bright spark must have thought: Hey! Elastic! Not just on knickers but on bottom sheets. No rucked-up knickers, so no rucked-up sheets. Brilliant! The "fitted" sheet had been invented.

Another persisting Dumbo-ism is corks in wine bottles. Decades after every other drink producer has given up using corks, the wine makers go on with this outdated practice. As well as being a tiresome bore to take out, the corks can also rot.

"Ai say, waitah, Ai'm afraid this wane is cawked."

Then order one with a screw top, dumbo. And get back to the caves.

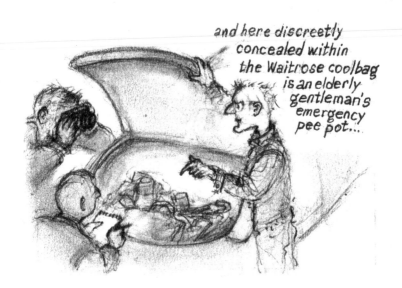

and here discreetly concealed within the Waitrose coolbag is an elderly gentleman's emergency pee pot...

Has the world gone mad?

OR IS IT just my bit? Over the last few years, I've been making a list of DAFT THINGS ASKED TO DO. Here are just a few.

Reputable publisher asks me to write a few entries in their Guide to Children's Books. They will pay £8.40 per entry! Hmm... not bad, I suppose. If I did ten it would help towards the plumber's bill for the tap.

Give a lecture on the work of a contemporary artist whose work I admire, but know almost nothing about. Lecture to be delivered in two weeks' time in *ABERDEEN! Fee £150*. Well, I suppose it might help with the rail fare.

Asked to send original artwork from a book published in 1961 to an exhibition in Gateshead. The artwork, if I could ever find it, is *49 years old* – dusty, faded, yellowing and worm-eaten; which I suppose might lend a certain period charm?

Japanese film producer asks for a meeting with me in London *on Boxing Day!* Well, say no more – foreigners. They live in another world.

A Scottish TV company sends TV contracts for my book, *UG*, *three months before the book is published!* They haven't even seen the book, let alone negotiated. I did think of asking for £50,000 cash in a brown envelope.

Asked by the *Mail on Sunday* to do a strip cartoon about the then current terrorist situation in the style of my book, *WHEN THE WIND BLOWS. Wanted by the end of the week!* The book took more than two years of full-time work.

Asked by Radio 4 programme, *The World This Weekend*, to take part in a discussion about terrorism, with the American Ambassador and others. Now that is true madness. Me and the American Ambassador: "Hi, Hank! How ya doin', pal?" I know Americans prefer an informal approach so I suppose it might have fitted in quite well.

Asked by *Sunday Times Magazine* to appear in a feature with Angela Barrett entitled "How We Met". We haven't met.

Asked by *Daily Telegraph* to take their motoring correspondent and a photographer out for a drive in my car and be *interviewed about my motoring!* "Well, yes, I get into the car, see? Then I turn the key, that starts the engine, then... um, I put it in gear, change up two or three times like so... and drive to where I'm going... then, when I get there, I apply the brake pedal, see? The car slows down and stops. I open the door, thus – and get out. That's about it, I'm afraid."

When I said no to this piffle, I was asked instead to take part in their feature called "Under The Lid", where I would be photographed and interviewed about *the contents of my car boot!* And they talk about the importance of having a free press! For what?

The new Head of Children's Picture Books at a publishers writes to introduce herself. Her letter begins: 'Dear Louise...'

Well, perhaps these people know more about my inner self than I do. It'll be all over the papers soon: SNOWMAN IN SEX-CHANGE ROMP.

England's green and potty land

DO WE KNOW how many potty people there are wandering about in our pleasant land? I have not met many of them, but here are just a few I have come across.

Once, I was in the Brighton library looking into a horizontal showcase when I happened to glance across at the queue of people waiting to check out their books. I caught the eye of a short, dumpy old woman in black who seemed to be staring fixedly at me.

I thought no more about it and went on looking into the case, but I must have felt her relentless gaze because, once again, I glanced across at the queue. There she was, still staring at me almost malevolently – her beady little brown eyes, hard as ball-bearings. I turned away and walked over to the door. I had just opened it when she appeared at my elbow, staring up at me with hatred in her eyes. "Swoine!" she hissed, "SWOINE!"

Politely, I held the door open for her and she went out, turning left for the main entrance.

I followed her but turned sharp right and hurried downstairs to the safety and sanity of the Gents.

Some time later, I was looking in a shop window in the Lanes, when I felt a tremendous kick in my ankle. I let out a howl, almost fell over, and had to steady myself by spreading my hands on the window.

I looked round and there, hurrying away into the crowd, was a short, dumpy old woman. Was it the same one?

Then one evening after a day's teaching, I went out for a peaceful walk along the seafront. I turned into a Gents and stood at the nearest urinal; at the other end of the empty row was what appeared to be an old tramp, puffing vigorously on a fag.

Suddenly, a cubicle door opened and out sprang a skinny but respectable elderly gent – neat, short greying hair and beard, polished black toecap shoes, neatly laced, and bright-blue ankle socks – stark naked. He skipped about on the wet concrete floor, clutching his private parts in both hands, turning and twisting as if on stage. Then

suddenly, he disappeared into the cubicle again. The old tramp looked across at me and said, "Do you want to do anything with him?" "No," I said, hastily buttoning my coat and making for the exit.

Now, have you ever had a stalker? I have and I would not recommend it.

One day, there was a knock at the door: student-age chap: "Hello, Raymond," he said, handing me a few sheets of A4. "Like you to read this, tell me what you think." "OK," I said. "How do I get it back to you?" "Oh, stick it on a post, halfway up the next footpath. How do I get to the station?" Later, I read the pages and wrote a polite note, saying it was OK, but as it was partly a children's book and partly a political satire it might be difficult to get it published. I then put it into a plastic bag, walked halfway up the Downs and pinned it to a post.

Then the nightmare began. His great obsession in life was to tell everyone about the 3,000 million starving people in the world. This, mixed up with guilt, sin and God, was what his writing was about, but he needed help from Bob Geldof. So could he have Bob Geldof's phone number?

Time and time again, over the

following two weeks, I told him I did not have Bob Geldof's phone number. Why on earth would I? This dispute went on and on, until one day I came home to find a large human turd on my doorstep. It was crawling with fat, green bluebottles and the whole front garden was littered with soiled lavatory paper. This is getting serious, I thought, if he can do that, anything is possible, even physical violence. So I called the police.

Two large policewomen turned up in their yellow reflector jackets, bristling with equipment. They seemed to fill the whole room. They duly inspected the turd, but were suddenly called away on a more important matter.

As they got into their car, one of them turned and said, "Have you really got Bob Geldof's phone number?"

The joy of bodkins

BODKINS. YESTERDAY, I used a bodkin for the first time in my life of over seventy years. Such a brilliant tool! How have I survived all these decades without once using a bodkin? I had heard of them of course, but had never seen one. In my mind they were associated with the elaborate garments of Victorian matrons – bodices, bustles and lace, shored up by colossal armoured corsets. That's where bodkins came in. Also, they were associated with crime, murder in particular, but

that was probably because of Dr John Bodkin Adams who, once again, specialised in elderly ladies.

I've always thought that for a desert island, the most vital tool is, of course, a knife, but my second choice would always be a long, thin metal tool with a sharp point. There are so many tasks where nothing else will do. But the bodkin is even better; it is long, thin, pointed and, incredibly, the point has a tiny hook on its end. So the bodkin can be inserted into a tightly closed gap, and hook something trapped inside and draw it out. Salvation! Brilliant! Nothing else in the world could do such a thing.

We were trying to help an elderly neighbour who had got the tapes fastening the hood of her winter coat into impossible knots. So, in this freezing weather, she couldn't use her hood. I tried for over a quarter of an hour – using two screwdrivers, a bradawl, dividers and knitting needles to probe into these fiendish knots, finally in a frenzy of frustration hurling the coat onto the floor.

Luckily, the lady was still in her own house at the time.

Then Liz suggested her grandmother's work basket, an ancient leather-topped box full of reels, ribbons, needles, pins, and a set of beautiful Victorian ivory-handled tools, one of which was a BODKIN! By comparison, Tutankhamen's Tomb was peanuts.

The whole job was done in less than four minutes.

But Liz's grandmother was born over 130 years ago, in 1881. Do young ladies today have work baskets? Will they be able to sew a button on hubby's trousers? Would they know a bodkin if they saw one? If they did see one, would they know what to do with it?

What will be the future of the human race in a world without bodkins?

P.S. Thinking I had better check my bodkin facts, I phoned Liz's grandchildren. The boy, 14, thought I was mental. The girls, 18 and 16, to my amazement, in the midst of their a-levels, iPods, smart phones, boy bands, CDs, DVDs, podcasts, MP3 players and Unis, both have sewing baskets! One of them makes her own 'tops', the other does embroidery

WITWCT? What is The World Coming To? How will these dreamy girlies ever come to terms with the modern world if they while away their youth fiddling about with needles and thread?

Still, neither of them knew what a bodkin was. So there.

The Whispering Gallery & VD

VENEREAL DISEASE CAST a shadow over my adolescence and no doubt over thousands of other teenagers at the time. Having had not one word of sex education at primary or secondary school, and not a single word from my parents, my complete ignorance made me vulnerable to every suggestion and rumour.

Throughout the Forties, there were posters everywhere showing the huge letters V and D casting dark shadows across the faces of young servicemen and women. They were quite frightening. To a thirteen-year-old who knew nothing whatever about either the sex or the disease, anything was possible. Had I got it? I used to lie awake at night, focussing my mind on the letters V and D and imagining the words YES or NO floating towards me, hoping for some sort of answer.

Then my friend Pfeff and I came across a small booklet in a newsagent's called *The Red Light*. It told you all about IT, not just about the disease, but IT as well. The booklet cost one and ninepence, so Pfeff and I agreed to form a joint company and to invest tenpence ha'penny each. We then tossed a coin and the loser had the embarrassing ordeal of entering the shop and asking for this shameful volume. Pfeff lost and so emerged from the shop, scarlet in the face, but triumphantly clutching the booklet.

We were in Fleet Street at the time, so we walked up to St Paul's and sat in one of the pews to read the book.

Syphilis you get a discharge... (an older boy at school had told me that if you get stuff coming out of it you've got VD...) gonorrhoea you get a sore... but then we were suddenly filled with joy: we couldn't have it because we hadn't done IT! You had to do IT to get it. Hooray! We were OK! We thumped one another on the shoulders and bounced up and down on our seats.

An attendant came over and glowered at us as he thought we were larking about. So we crept away like good little boys and walked sedately towards the Whispering Gallery. Until that moment, I had had no idea that Pfeff had VD worries as well. We'd probably both been too embarrassed to even mention it to one another.

We climbed a long way up the narrow stone staircase, then an even narrower passage led off to the left, with a rope across it saying NO ENTRY. Naturally, we ducked under the rope and went on and up. This led to a heavy door which we pushed open. When we stepped outside, we found ourselves on the roof of the nave; the huge towers in front of us and the massive dome above us. After the dark narrow passage, the space and dazzling light were almost frightening, but with the birds wheeling around in the blue sky, it was exhilarating too. We ran about all over the enormous roof, bigger than our school playground, waving our arms at the birds.

The space! The light! We're on top of St Paul's! And we haven't got VD!

BREATHE THROUGH YOUR SKULL!
ACUPUNCTURE!
IMAGINE YOU ARE A TREE!
TRY ORIENTAL DANCING!
EAT MORE MAGNESIUM!
GIVE UP COFFEE!
CARESS YOUR FEET!
DON'T EAT TOO MUCH!
DO YOGA!
GIVE UP DRINK!
THE DOG POSITION!
QI GONG!

Stress relief

Who is normal?

AM I GOING POTTY? Or is it just my friends who are potty? Who is normal? What is normal?

We have just been to visit two old friends, who are our exact contemporaries. Despite their colossal age, they have recently moved into an apartment in a newly converted Victorian rectory. Now, is that potty? Yes, to me it's insane. To move house in your eighties!

They are the first people to occupy it, so everything was spotless and brand new – dazzling white floors, gleaming brass and polished woodwork everywhere. It made my brain ache. I needed my dark

glasses but they were in the car, and it seemed rude to go out and get them, and if I'd worn them indoors, they might think I'd gone potty. When we went into the immaculate sitting room, I gazed awestruck at the exquisitely arranged sofa – two perfect cushions, tipped up onto their corners, making a double diamond shape next to one another, the space between them carefully judged. At first, I dared not sit down in case my elbow accidently made a crease in a cushion. But eventually, I took the plunge. Don't spill the coffee! screeched a voice in my head, as I lowered myself into the billowing depths. Once sunken in, I felt I might never get out again.

But then we were shown into the two bedrooms. Oh no! Not more immaculate perfection, surely? But yes, there it was – like an ultra-posh country hotel. Nothing on the bedside tables except one lamp, discreetly shaded and impossible to read by. Nothing else at all, and they were living in these rooms! They appeared to be completely unoccupied. No clock, no radio, no pen, no pencil, no notepad, no phone. Above all, no books! Even in a hotel you get the Bible. Don't they read in bed? Wake up in the night and need to write themselves a note, a reminder? Or listen to the radio, to stay sane and relate to the rest of the world, run by John Humphrys?

Arriving home, I went straight up to look at my own bedside table. This is a two-drawer filing cabinet boxed in with plywood. Oh dear! Not at all immaculate. Pocket notebook, two propelling pencils, several pens, red, blue and black, RNIB clock – ultra-clear, thermometer with indoor and outdoor temperatures, torch, landline phone, mobile phone, Snowman night light (a gentle glow instead of 60 watts), my first Anglepoise lamp from 1958 (60 watts), glasses, optical lens wipes, eye shade with peak, blackout eye shades for daytime dozing (a siesta is vital), woolly hat for cold nights, handkerchief and box of tissues. Not clutter, all in use.

Then, the BOOKS. Fourteen of them. Now that's where there is, perhaps, a degree of pottiness. One of them is *Stress Relief*. Haven't read it yet; been too stressed to open it. Will have a quick look now – Ah... they recommend ZEN & ZAZEN. Must nip down the chemist, see if they've got any.

It's all best summed up by Jeanette Winterson's extraordinary book with the brilliant title *Why Be Happy When You Could Be Normal?* Well, I'm certainly not happy, so perhaps after all I am normal.

P.S. Just realised this could have been resolved earlier by looking at a 1998 note on the wall here. Today, during a lull in the conversation, Connie (3½years old) looked across at me and said, "Raymond is not a normal person." Brilliant! Three-and-a-half! The best compliment I've ever had. It's going on my tombstone.

Sit down, Mum.

I don't like this table. Your mother always sits here.

God's waiting room

HAVING IN A previous article made light of the new chums that often come to live with you in old age just as your old friends are drifting away – Al Zeimers, Pa Kinson, D. Mensher, etc. – I'm beginning to wish I'd never written it.

Several old friends have got in touch to tell me that there are at least six of our contemporaries who are enduring visits from these long-term, live-in chums. One chap has Alzheimer's; he still manages to live alone, but is looked after several times a week by his son and daughters. Another is still at work, but has Parkinson's. A third has advanced Parkinson's now sliding into dementia. Another had had Parkinson's for a long time, but died last year. Two more have been in care homes for several years now.

I was particularly shocked to hear about one of these, as she was a very attractive, lively girl and virtually a teenage nymphomaniac. At one time she was even after me! Unbelievable. But I was a nervous teenage virgin at the time; not only that, she was married. That really finished me off.

I knew her husband quite well and the thought of DOING IT with his wife, then coming face to face with him, socially, afterwards was unthinkable. DOING IT at all made me nervous, but DOING IT with someone's wife rendered me doubly impotent. I remember one evening walking with her to the station after the failure of my second attempt and she said: "I'll get you one day."

Blimey! Those were the days! Pity it's too late now. Where have they gone – all those nymphomaniacs?

It also turns out that one of our contemporaries has been, for many years, living only a few miles away. He is now in a care home too, so, although we were not close, I thought I ought to go and see him.

It was quite a grand building, set in its own grounds – almost a stately home. He was in a large sitting room with a wide-screen television and eight or nine other residents sitting around in huge armchairs with tip-up leg rests. We recognised one another – just – after a gap of over half a century.

I suppose it must be because I look so young. He, by contrast, was a very old man indeed.

He looked strained, tense and preoccupied, as if he was not fully present. Two or three other residents were even more strained. One lady, tall and elegant, had an expression of intense grief, mouth wide open in an agony of silent sobbing, both hands constantly twitching the hem of her dress. I have visited three times now and she is always in the same endlessly agonised state.

Another resident is a big strong man with powerful, tanned arms – very heavily built and not frail or ancient at all; he looks to be no more than 60. He is always unconscious, never moves, not even turning his head towards the television. Never speaks.

Both of these people are hoisted off their seats by an electrically operated harness and pushed across the room on a trolley to the dining table, where they are lowered into their chairs. On the way, they hang in their harness, swinging about like a sack of potatoes.

Yesterday, someone said these places are called God's Waiting Room. Well, we're all in that already, aren't we?

P.S. In the midst of writing this, an old friend, who I haven't spoken to for well over a year, phoned to say she could no longer drive. I didn't ask why, and made some jokey remark about the joys of old age, saying I was 80 last month. Well, she said, I've only got two months to go. We chatted on for a couple of minutes, then she said: How old are you?

That evening, her son phoned to say his mum had been having memory tests as she is getting dementia.

DATES
to the rescue!

WHEN THE FAMILY SWEET COUPONS are exhausted and the children threaten to raid the sugar bowl, that's the moment to produce a packet of dates. Solid food and no stones, every packet contains a wealth of good energy food and is an immediate answer to that craving for "something sweet".

THE MINISTRY OF FOOD, LONDON, S.W.1.

Long ago and not so far away

THE PAST IS another country: we did things differently when we were there.

*THE RADIO TIMES JOURNAL
OF THE BBC
PRICE TWOPENCE*

*PROGRAMMES FOR
AUG 27 – SEPT 2 1950
TELEVISION EDITION*

Yellowed, tattered and torn (like the BBC today), the cover shows a black and white photograph of an elderly chap in a woolly pullover, wearing glasses, with a strap for headphones above his furrowed brow. He has one finger to his lips and is gazing down intently at a tangle of wires, knobs and notebooks. He is implying "Shush! Listen…" It is the great Ludwig Koch.

This is in contrast to a recent cover showing a woman with her bosom thrust forward and some bloke behind her with his hand, fingers widespread, hovering inches away from it.

Oh, dear. Sad, a yoof would say.

Inside, a new high-tech miracle

is announced: "First Television Programme from the Other Side of the Channel. On Sunday evening, BBC Television reaches out from the land across the sea for the first programme to be televised direct from the Continent."

My! All that way... all 22 miles "from the land across the sea"... almost as far as Guildford.

Then, there is a panel: THIS WEEK IN TELEVISION: 7 lines, 5 programmes. The panel is $2^1/_2$ inches wide and 1 inch deep.

The advertising is from another country, too. 'DATES TO THE RESCUE!' A picture of two grinning children, each clutching a solid block of dates the size of half a brick, and chomping into it as if it was a giant choc-ice. "THE MINISTRY OF FOOD, LONDON, SW1"

"He stands at the Cross Roads": rear view of a naked, chubby infant standing at a suburban crossroads; his left arm towards a skinny youth in long trousers, hands in pockets, head drooping. His right arm towards a rugged, muscley man in white shorts, legs braced apart... "The choice is yours. COW & GATE The Food of ROYAL BABIES."

Well, my mum let me down there – I'm certainly the skinny, droopy-head one. So now, at 80, am I too late for Cow & Gate?

Then there was the strange mania for so-called cowboy music:

Sunday

8.20 Johnny Dent and his Ranchers; Graham Bailey and the Cactus Kids.

3.45 Big Bill's PRAIRIE ROUND UP – Old Cabin Favourites including Buck Douglas, The Old Cowpuncher; Jimmy Hawthorn, The Yodelling Buckaroo; The Bunkhouse Boys and Big Bill Campbell.

But, worst of all, were those infernal, everlasting ORGANS! Day after day. Having suffered in the cinema with my mum and dad, when we had gone to the Tooting Granada, to see a film; between the A film and the second feature, a hideous monstrosity eerily rose out of the floor, lit up from inside – pink, green and yellow and emitting an excruciating noise. A man in a black bow tie and white jacket spun round on his plastic stool and beamed at his captive audience.

Were it not for the deafening 'music' you could have heard

the groans all around, everyone knowing they now had to endure twenty minutes of this torture.

But masochists could always turn to the *Radio Times*.

Sunday

10.15: Sandy MacPherson at the BBC Theatre Organ

Monday

10.00: Neville Meale at the BBC Theatre

9.00: At the electric organ, Ron Millington from the Winter Gardens, Bournemouth

Wednesday

10.00: Charles Smitton at the BBC Theatre Organ

Thursday

4.30: Sandy MacPherson at the BBC Theatre Organ

Friday

3.00: Lloyd Thomas at the BBC Theatre Organ

10.00: Robinson Cleaver at the organ of the Granada Tooting.

AAAGH! NO! NO! NO! Not that one! Enough! Stop now!

The organ grinds on

SIR: Raymond Briggs in his Notes From the Sofa roundly condemned the cinema organ both in appearance and sound. I would like to inform him that the cinema organ is alive and well and has a strong following, not just in this country but all over the world.

I wonder whether Mr Briggs would like to get up from his sofa and come to listen anew to a cinema organ concert; such organs are playing merrily all around the country in a variety of venues since they left the cinemas. There are one or two still in situ, such as at the Odeon Leicester Square and the Curzon Cinema in Weston-super-Mare, but others can be found in a variety of venues such as town halls, amusement parks, churches and even in people's houses.

Music played on cinema organs tends to appeal to those of slightly more advancing years, although there are many up-and-coming young players, too. In fact, in July a competition took place to find the Young Theatre Organist of the Year. I feel sure the cinema organ will be played for many more years to come.

Sarah Bryant, Whitstable, Kent

PEACE & QUIET

IN the Seventies we used to have holidays in an isolated stone cottage on a pebble beach in Kirkcudbrightshire. The sea came to within yards of the door.

It was very primitive with no heating except for a ruinous old range. There was tap water and a lavatory, but no electricity or lighting. The nearest road was a mile away.

The calls of curlews and oystercatchers filled the air.

A fisherman who lived nearby caught salmon and we used to cook them on the range over a fire of driftwood.

The two children were 12 and 10 at the time and we all spent the time happily swimming, drawing and painting, walking and just wandering about.

No traffic, no television, no radio, no phone.

Peace and quiet. Paradise.

Raymond Briggs

My shooting times

SHOOTING WAS FORCED upon me by my being, at one time, a dedicated gardener.

Trying to grow your own vegetables whilst living on the lower slopes of the South Downs is a nightmare. The entire landscape is infested with rabbits, sometimes you can see thirty or forty at a time.

I did all the right things – bought seed trays, the correct John Innes seed compost, dampened perfectly, kept the trays in the kitchen for gentle warmth, and, when the seeds had sprouted, put the trays in the light on the windowsill, turning them round once or twice a day so the plants didn't stretch to the light. Later, I took them out to the large, expensive cold frame with its own built-in watering system, dug over the veg patch again, then hoed and raked it to perfection. A few days later, the great moment came – with garden line, stretched straight... bedding out could begin!

All plants spaced correctly, the recommended distance apart. Done! Success!

Next morning, go up to see how the plants are... Gone! Nothing at all. Not even a chewed stump.

These stupid rabbits have the entire South Downs to feed on, millions of different plants of all flavours, and the buggers have to come down and gobble up mine!

I tried the old idea of fencing the veg patch with wire mesh, but this has to be buried at least a foot below the surface. Quite a laborious, boring job and they still get in anyway.

So, nothing for it, shoot the buggers. Got a Russian Baikal single-barrel shot gun, very cheap (through the post in those days!) I then used to keep a record of the number shot each day and, as the months went by, the total came to over 200.

It made no difference whatsoever. You do become incredibly callous. I used to hang the rabbits, skin them and eat them – cooked of course. I once saw two, almost baby, rabbits crouched together in a slight hollow. They'll be delicious, I thought. BANG! Both dead from one shot (an ace marksman). They were completely tasteless.

Another time, a friend and I came home after a day's teaching, and we wandered into the garden with glasses of wine. As I stepped out of the french window, I trod on a rabbit. Before it could run, I dived down, grabbed it and killed it with my bare hands. Filled with such hatred, I even forgot about the wine. My friend was quite shocked, but being a gardener himself, he understood.

But then, sometimes your own pre-rabbit humanity surfaces again. Quite often, a rabbit will be hit by the shot but not killed – the back legs are paralysed and they continue to run, using their weak little front paws and dragging their useless back legs behind them. You can't shoot them again at such short range; as it would blow them to bits, so I used to go over and knock them on the head with the butt of the gun. Once, doing this, the rabbit saw me coming and let out a scream of fear like a human baby. I had no idea rabbits had a voice. It was quite chilling.

Another time, I was walking down a hill, when a pigeon flew over. Why, I don't know, I whipped up the gun and shot it. When I found it, the poor creature was lying on its back, wings spread out, feebly fluttering – its beak opening and closing soundlessly. No doubt it was in great pain. I cried. That finished my shooting times for ever.

P.S. Once, in the early days of my shooting career, friends at the pub invited me to join them in a 'Clay Shoot'. This is where someone catapults clay 'pigeons' into the air and you take pot shots at them. I failed to hit a single one, so I was awarded a long wooden spoon with a miniature bottle of gin tied to it with a pretty ribbon – the Booby Prize. I should have taken the hint there and then.

Individuality

WE ARE ALL individual, aren't we? Of course we are, it's unarguable, isn't it?

In the Painting Class at Wimbledon Art School, we all had our individual styles. You could walk into a room hung with our work and tell instantly who had painted each picture. Each of us was unique, or so we thought.

Then later, in the very first week at the Slade School, I was in a corridor showing my paintings to a couple of newfound friends. Just then, another new student walked by, whom I had not seen before. He paused slightly, glanced down at my work and said: "Wimbledon?" and passed on without waiting for a reply.

Just as well he didn't, as I was too stunned to speak. He could tell at a glance that I was from Wimbledon Art School! It was unbelievable. How could 20 or so of us have one easily recognisable style when we were all so different from one another, so individual?

Could it be that we were not individuals at all? Had we all

been sheep, herded through the Wimbledon academic art factory? A product with our brand name stamped on us?

But more was to come. A year later there was a combined Slade/ Royal College exhibition. Now at the Slade, unlike Wimbledon, there was a multitude of styles, from Coldstream's measuring Realism, through Expressionism and every 'ism' under the sun, to hard-edge Abstraction. Every individual was painting in a completely different style of art.

Yet, you could stand in the doorway of the gallery and tell from yards away which paintings came from which school. The Slade pictures were more colourful, much happier and more human. RCA work was huge, grim, abstract and inhuman. But, of course, all the students believed they were individuals who had their own personal style.

My stuff didn't get into that exhibition. Too individual, I expect.

Neville Heath's waxwork in Madame Tussaud's

Up and on!

DO THEY STILL have school songs? I hope not, not if they are anything like my old school song: 'Up boys! Truest fa-a-ame lies in high end-deav-our! Up boys! Play the game! Up and on!'

Oh dear... it's even more embarrassing today, over sixty years later. Of course, we all had a slightly different interpretation of 'Up and On' to the one the writer intended. All this was brought to mind by reading the superb biography of Neville George Clevely Heath: *Handsome Brute*

by Sean o'Connor; a tremendous piece of detailed and moving research. Oldies will remember that Heath's appalling murders were two of the vilest ever known.

The years was 1946. The whole country was horrified but fascinated by the story, particularly me and my thirteen-year-old chums at Rutlish in Merton, because it was Heath's old school. At lunchtimes we all rushed out to buy the papers and read the latest dreadful details.

Looking back now on those olden days, I wonder if he would

be as successful with today's young women as he was then? He was extremely good-looking, so that would still work, but he put on a posh accent and fantasised about his supposed posh background – Eton, Oxford, etc. Would that cut much ice today? Modern young women might think him a pompous, old-fashioned snob. In post-war England too, women were also wowed by uniforms: 'Mummy! He's a Flying officer!'

Uniforms are long gone and the very occupation of pilot has lost its glamour. Airline pilots now are no more glamorous than bus drivers, sitting in their cabins watching a video while a computer does the flying and the co-pilot's children trot in and out to chat to daddy. The glamorous fighter pilot's work now seems to be done by drones guided by chaps sitting at desks thousands of miles away from the targets. When they knock off and pop home to the missus and kids, they must sometimes wonder how many people they have killed since lunch.

A legendary former headmaster of Rutlish, Mr Varnish, had written a Speech Book, which instructed us how to talk posh. It was compulsory to carry it in your left-hand blazer pocket; if a pre or a sub caught you without it: automatic detention. Mr Varnish had gone by my day, but I wonder what he would have felt if he had known that his Speech Book had helped groom Heath into poshness, and so assisted him in his deceptions and crimes.

The appalling effect of such murders – both committed in a few minutes – lingers on for decades. Heath's own family – mother, father, brother, wife and son – the families of the victims; their lives were blighted for ever by the horror.

Up and On? Well, the rope certainly went up, and the white hood went on, then Pierrepoint slipped back the catch, the trap fell open, and Heath was down and gone. Truest fame? Well, a life-size waxwork in Madame Tussaud's Chamber of Horrors is more than most of us old Ruts can expect. Thank heavens!

Snow sadists: me and Hannibal

"FOR THE SHEER number of little hearts broken in one summary execution, writer Briggs must stand high on the league table of snow sadists – rather like Hannibal."

Golly! I must say I never thought I would see my name in the same sentence as little broken hearts, summary execution, sadists and Hannibal. Still, there it is in print, in the *Evening Standard* and written by Charles Saatchi, no less.

I can only think it is part of a cunning plan of his to lure me into doing Art Paintings again and

selling them in his gallery. Huge, sploshy, dribbling oils – pictures of sobbing infants half-buried in snow drifts being menaced by herds of trumpeting elephants, urged on by Hannibal and me waving gigantic icicles like spears. Saatchi must have researched my spectacular career in the Arts, and was so impressed he devised this ruse.

In 1951, after two years at Wimbledon Art School and at the age of seventeen, I was awarded the Intermediate Art Certificate (my mum framed it). This allowed me to proceed for a further two years and to be awarded the National Diploma of Design (in Painting) – the NDD. This was followed by two years in the army in Catterick. Here, I did an Art Painting entitled *3am on the Catterick Flyer*, the weekly midnight train from King's Cross –, packed with fellow conscripts getting back to Catterick after their 36-hour weekend pass. This was exhibited in the Young Contemporaries Show at the RBA Galleries, where it was sold and also well-reviewed by the great John Berger, who wrote for the *New Statesman*.

Saatchi must have researched all this and seen that here was a potential gold mine.

It made me dig out my 'Scrap Album' for 1955 (only 59 years ago) where the first two stained and yellowing press cuttings in it were the only Art Painting reviews I've ever had. From then on, the cuttings are all about baby books and nursery rhymes, not Great Art.

Berger writes: '...whilst out of the hundred or so everyday scenes, accepted simply for their banality, there is one that arrests because it has been seen with passion, with concern – *3am on the Catterick Flyer* by Raymond Briggs. Here, in front of soldiers uncouthly sprawling asleep on a train, one is moved – tenderly – by the commonplace, because of all that wells up behind but never over it. With its ferocious foreshortenings, disarrayed composition and raw colour, this picture is also to some degree a reaction against the convention of Art. Yet it is justified because it is a reaction against the inadequacy of that convention for a definite purpose. Of what use is Caravaggio in a city of fluorescent lighting? Of what use even the heroics of Picasso in front of the puppy dreams of khaki conscripts? And it is, of course, by asking just such questions that the convention is re-established. Caravaggio and Picasso asked them in their time, and Briggs pays his respects, proves that his questions are not arrogant, in another painting – a faithful adaptation of a Renaissance Pietà. Many other students could learn from these two pictures how to make use of their suspicion and scepticism.'

Golly gosh! First, me, sadists and Hannibal, then me, Caravaggio and Picasso! My cup runneth over. It went all down my trousers (again!).

Whatever next? I'd better retire now before it gets any worse.

Ladies only

COMING ACROSS THIS photograph recently in a dusty file, I wondered where it had come from: old bloke in a flat cap, baggy trousers and shiny boots... pre-war, surely? It took me some time to remember that it could have only been me who had taken it, so it was probably not pre-war, as I was four years old then. It took even longer for me to believe that I had taken it. Above all, when? Eventually, it dawned on me that it must have been in the very early Sixties. Well, that's not long ago, is it? Beatles

and all that – 1963? Yesterday... Get the calculator... can't do mental arithmetic any more... 2014–1961 = 53. Fifty-three years ago! Over half a century! Ye Gods! No wonder the photograph looks old. I must have been a yoof of 27.

Behind the old (?) bloke's flat cap, on the wall, is a sign: POST OFFICE LONDON DIRECTORY FOR REFERENCE PHONE YOUR ENQUIRIES TO TEMPLE BAR 3464. Ah! The days when telephone exchanges had names! WIMbledon, SLOane, HAMpstead, and the legendary WHItehall one two one two. There is also the lower half of a sign saying ONLY. This is almost certainly LADIES ONLY outside the LADIES WAITING ROOM. And yes, yoof, there were LADIES ONLY compartments on the trains, too. These compartments had two rows of four seats and a door each side. There were no corridors, so once inside you were trapped in until the next stop. So ladies felt safer, in case they were alone in a compartment and someone nasty got in.

I've never read enough feminist writing to know how they felt about the Ladies Only idea, but they were probably passionately against it. Patronising? Demeaning? However, it could be seen as a compliment, regarding them as special.

If there were compartments labelled 80-YEAR-OLD ILLUSTRATORS ONLY, I'd be in there like a shot. At least I'd be sure of getting a seat. Men only, of course. No young, nosy Posy Simmondses poking in, thank you.

Oddest of all, is the little boy almost cuddling up to the rough-looking man, who is bemused

by this. It is clear that they are not together, let alone related, so where were the little boy's parents? If this happened today, the man would not sit there, relaxed and bemused, he would leap up and be gone before the paedophilia police arrived.

But for today, what about a sign: GAYS ONLY? How would that go down? Or LESBIANS ONLY? HOMOSEXUALS ONLY?

It all gets slightly complicated. Even before we mention HETEROS ONLY, let alone BISEXUALS or INTERS. As a HETERO, broadly speaking, I might quite like a HETEROS ONLY compartment, just in case there was a marauding Lesbian nympho lurking, eager to broaden her horizons.

But maybe we shouldn't label people at all?

My only experience of LADIES ONLY was rushing on to the platform at Wimbledon station one morning – flags waving, whistles blowing, train moving, grabbed the nearest handle, opened door, scrambled in, slammed door. Carriage full of ladies – eight sitting, three standing, wafts of perfume... Oh, oh sorry... a few titters... Getting out Clapham Junction... sorry...

The train stopped at Earlsfield and I moved to get out, but an eagle-eyed railway man espied me, came over, flung open the door and said, "Any objections to this cockerel in the 'en run?"

Laughter all round.

Root of the problem

SIR: I never thought my family lore would illustrate an article in *The Oldie* (Notes From the Sofa: 'Ladies only') but my aunt's adventure before the First World War does just that. As a young woman, she found herself alone in a compartment in a corridor-less train. Just before the train moved off, a man carrying a raw turnip jumped in and sat opposite her. When the train was well under way he produced a large knife, cut a slice of turnip, stuck it on the end of the knife, pushed it nearly into her face and commanded "Eat!" No corridor, no alarm, no hope of help – just the man, the knife and the turnip. The terrified girl took the turnip and munched. She had chewed her way through three slices of raw turnip before the train came to a halt and she hurled herself onto the platform.

Unlikely as it seems this story explains why 'ladies only' compartments were not to be laughed at and why turnip was never served in my grandparents' house.

A Watson, Hexham, Northumberland

Art-class art and class

IS SOCIAL SNOBBERY dying out, or does it just attach itself to different things?

Pre-war magazines were full of advertisements for products recommended by the aristocracy: "Lady Felicity Fitz-Phartasse always uses Splond's Vanishing Cream." Such an advertisement today would have people helpless with laughter. But now it is the celebs who recommend products. They are the new aristocracy and no one is laughing.

In the Forties, a boy at school asked: "Is your bath filled in at the sides?" "Yes," I lied. Filled-in sides meant modern, middle-class, while a bare bath meant out-of-date, lower-class. Today, it is the reverse – filled in means suburban, out-of-date.

"How many houses are there in your street, Briggo?" "Oh, I don't know... about a hundred, I suppose." "A HUNDRED! Bloody hell!" We lived in an Edwardian terrace house, while most boys came from further out in the Surrey suburbs, and lived in 1930s semis with garages.

Now the snobbery is reversed. Those Edwardian terraces, soon to be a hundred years old, have period charm and are more desirable than the semis.

In the early fifties, I once went with my mum and dad to the Royal Academy Summer Show. We went into the Academy café for a cup of tea. Immediately, a head waiter bore down upon us, complete with black tie, gleaming collar and cuffs, looking very unwelcoming. My poor parents almost panicked, and mumbled some excuse. We turned and fled. Now, pictures of David Cameron dolled up in fancy gear as a member of some toffs-only club in Oxford make him a laughing stock. Him? A leader? A Prime Minister?

The snobbery is reversed, but the greatest reversal has come in accents. At grammar school we had lessons teaching us how to talk posh. "THE LION CHASED THE UNICORN ALL AROUND THE TOWN," enunciated the master in his plummy voice. "De line chised de yoonikawn aller ranner tan," we echoed in our south suburban sub-cockney. Now, Ken Livingstone talks in the same accent with no discredit at all.

Not long ago, I heard a recording of John Lennon being interviewed by the BBC in the Sixties. The fluting poshness of the interviewer sounded ludicrous next to Lennon's down-to-earth Liverpudlian. In the last few years, even the Queen has tried to de-posh her accent, with some success. Recently, an interviewer mentioned my South London vowels. So the speech lessons don't seem to have done much good. I am still common. Common and proud of it! I am an inverted snob.

Healthy minds, healthy bodies

IN THE THIRTIES, there was an obsession with laxatives. "Inner cleanliness" was an advertising catch phrase. Every child was given a weekly dose, whether constipated or not. Mine was Syrup of Figs every Friday night. It was thin, vile and black, but not as vile as Milk of Magnesia which was thick, powdery and white.

Why was everyone doing this? No one does it today. How do these medical fads begin?

Is it marketing pressure from the manufacturers? Is it mild mass hysteria? Why do the fads eventually fade away?

Every week I also had to take a dessert spoonful of Radio Malt. Its sweet, toffee-like taste concealed the cod liver oil. The iron fist in a velvet glove. The label had a yellow sun with its rays shining from a sky blue background. What had the sun to do with Radio? What had cod liver oil to do with Radio? The jar was kept behind the mirror above the kitchen fireplace so the warmth would keep it pliable. When cold, it had the consistency of Blu-Tack.

Other children had Virol, which was similar, but my Mum thought was common. Most of us liked Radio Malt and Virol, as they were sweet and sticky and not like medicine at all.

These products were a huge commercial success, particularly Virol. Blue and orange Virol posters, usually of enamelled metal were everywhere and now are collectors' items. "Virol. Anaemic Girls Need It." "Virol. Delicate Chests Need It." They were even on the risers of the steps in railway stations. "Virol. Used in 3,000 Hospitals." Metal posters. They must have been very expensive to make and obviously intended to last for ever. Now they are long gone. Look upon my Virol posters, ye mighty, and despair. And where is Virol today? The nation needs to know!

What health fads taken seriously today will be laughable in fifty years' time? Aerobics is already on the way out. Jogging is also fading. What will be next? The craze for the gym? T'ai chi? Pilates? Prime candidates for oblivion must be feng shui and aromatherapy. It would be interesting to run a book on it. The Good For You Stakes.

Serious medical procedures have also come and gone. ECT is discredited now. In 1971, this was given to my dying mother, who was depressed because she was dying. Leuchotomy or pre-frontal lobotomy has gone already, thank God.

I can remember the blank-faced ladies sitting under the trees at the local mental hospital, with bandages round their heads where their skulls had been sawn through and their brains cut in two; the tears running down their cheeks.

GOOD DAY DAW!

Apoplectic Christmas opulence

CHARLES DICKENS IS a great writer. We all know that, but he certainly could do with some editing. He wouldn't survive long under the iron editorship of today's publishing houses.

Take this paragraph from *A Christmas Carol*: "There were great, round pot-bellied baskets of chesnuts, shaped like the waistcoats of jolly old gentlemen, lolling at the doors, and tumbling out into the street in their apoplectic opulence. There were ruddy, brown-faced, broad-girthed Spanish Onions, shining in the fatness of their growth like Spanish Friars; and winking from their shelves in wanton slyness at the girls as they went by..."

Blimey! Was he on something? Chesnuts (spelled wrong, but never mind), pot-bellied baskets shaped like waistcoats, lolling at doors, and apoplectic opulence!

Apoplectic opulence sums up

this writing quite well. Beginner writers are always being told to cut down on adjectives, yet Dickens uses six adjectives to describe onions, which most of us have seen before. And the onions are like lecherous Friars; well, that does sound remarkably up to date, so he did have foresight.

"...there were Norfolk Biffins, squab and swarthy, setting off the yellow of the oranges and lemons, and, in the great compactness of their juicy persons, urgently entreating and beseeching to be carried home..." They sound like illegal immigrants, except that they are "to be carried home in paper bags and eaten after dinner."

"...while the Grocer and his people were so frank and fresh that the polished hearts with which they fastened their aprons behind might have been their own, worn outside for general inspection, and for Christmas daws to peck at if they chose."

Aprons fastened with polished hearts? Couldn't they just tie a knot? Their own hearts for general inspection? Why? Jackdaws pecking at the back parts of grocers? This is borderline barmy. Almost time for the men in long white coats.

"The very gold and silver fish, set forth among these choice fruits in a bowl, though members of a dull and stagnant-blooded race, appeared to know that there was something going on; and, to a fish, went gasping round and round their little world in slow and passionless excitement."

Passionless excitement? *[Bit of a contradiction? Ed.]* Stagnant-blooded? *[They'd be dead wouldn't they? Ed.]* Went gasping? *[Fish? they don't breathe air, do they? Ed.]*

"...the candied fruits so caked and spotted with molten sugar as to make the coldest lookers-on feel faint and subsequently bilious." *[Quite. Say no more. Ed.]*

Where are you, Jess?

ON TUESDAY, I took our Border Collie, Jess, for her usual morning walk. She ran along the edge of the wood and all over the fields, full of her usual energy.

When we came back, she was just going through the doorway from the kitchen to the living room, when she gave a curious, repeated humping movement of her shoulders and back. She still had her harness on, so I thought she was trying to get it off. As I bent down to undo it, she suddenly collapsed; all four legs splayed out,

flat on the floor, her head on one side.

Liz and I knelt down, stroking her head and trying to wet her lips with water. I phoned our vet 5 times: always engaged. Phoned four dog-owning neighbours to ask for their vet's number. All out. Phoned our vet for the sixth time and they said bring her in.

She managed to walk up the long garden path, but I had to lift her into her bed in the boot. We got there in about half an hour and a vet assistant helped me to carry her in. She told me to take the head end so that Jess could see I was still with her.

The vet examined her, said he needed to do X-rays, if we could wait for a while. When he showed the X-rays on the wall, he said there was fluid round the lungs and the heart was not beating strongly enough to move it. She might have to go to a cardiologist which would cost several hundred pounds, or go to a clinic in Brighton overnight. But meanwhile, he would continue his own treatment to make her heart more responsive. Her heart had already improved slightly. She had been very cold when she came in, and now was warmer. He would phone us between four and five.

We sat near the phone all afternoon, waiting. When at last he rang, he said: I think we'll have to let her go.

Oh good, I said. We'll come in straight away. No, he said, I don't mean go home. Just let her go.

When this had finally sunk in, I said: We still want to see her. That's all right, he said.

So we went in again and found her lying on his table covered in a blue blanket. Her eyes were wide open and staring, but not looking. We stroked her head and talked to her, but even then, I was not sure if she was alive or dead.

When we got home, the house seemed empty and dead. I opened the cupboard to get something and there was the jug with her afternoon meal measured out. Her empty bowl was on the floor. Her empty bed still lies under the window behind the sofa. Her lead, harness, and red ball on a strong, still hang just inside the back door.

Shopping next day, I looked at the usual dog food shelves, Baker's compete, Dentastix, and Markies – her passion. No need for any of them ever again.

Today, Thursday, the vet phoned. Did we want her ashes to be returned to us today, or scattered? Scattered, please, I said.

So Jess, now you are powder and ash blown by the wind, somewhere in Sussex. That's all we know. You are not far away, but where are you, Jess?

OOOH! MINE!
A CUP OF COFFEE
AT LAST!

AND IT'S ONLY
£2,298·95!

Caffiends

I STILL CAN'T believe it, yet here it is in front of me. A forty-page magazine about coffee! It's called *Caffeine* – "the coffee lover's magazine". It is not for the trade but for us, the consumers. What on earth do we need to know about coffee? I'd much rather have a magazine about marmalade.

On the cover are nine photographs of cups of coffee in various bleak environments and only one of them has human beings in it, far away in the distant background, smaller than the coffee cup. A heading says: "FEEDING YOUR OBSESSION. Does Instagram offer more than endless photos of latte art?" Latte art? What in heaven's name is that? Marmaladart I could

just about tolerate.

Further joys are announced inside. There is to be a London Coffee Festival, held in trendy Brick Lane, in April. There is a dismal coffee-coloured Christmas card with a Festival offer for Caffeine readers: "2 VIP tickets for £70 (save £60)." I don't even understand that. I suppose it must be a joke.

The writing about coffee tasting reads very like wine babble: "Rich cherry flavour, mild lemon acidity, heavy, almost chewy, rich chocolate and malt, almond and juicy raisin flavours. It ends up tasting like a sweet, milky, hot chocolate." So why not have a sweet, milky, hot chocolate in the first place? Much cheaper.

Then there are BARISTAS. I'd vaguely heard the word before and thought it was Italian barristers, but no, it's a much more distinguished profession than a mere barrister, it is the title of someone whose profession is pouring hot water onto coffee grounds and thus making – wait for it... Yes. You've got it! COFFEE! Fantastic! There are also "Latte Art Championships where you see some of the country's best baristas compete". Sit and watch a few blokes making coffee? Why on earth?

One bar has created a drink "which is a blend of warmed cold brew, cranberry, sugar syrup and a sprinkle of Christmas spice in the form of cinnamon, nutmeg, clove and star anise." So why bother with coffee then?

In Stockholm, in the *Kaffeverket*, you could try a cappuccino made using Santa Rosa bean from Costa Rica, which employs a meticulous method of patio drying and revolutionary depulpers. I do believe in using a proper depulper, don't you? "The taste was wonderfully layered, beginning with pecan and ending with a burst of plum and lemon."

Well, why not have a nutty fruit salad and be done with it?

This nonsense was brought about by two friends who seemed obsessed with coffee. I used to silently count the number of times they mentioned it and eventually said "Do you realise that you two have said the word 'coffee' 27 times in the last hour and a half?" This became a family joke and is now referred to as "the C word". Later, they sent me the magazine to show they were not alone in this lunacy.

At Christmas I thought I would give them a piece of coffee-making equipment, but I soon changed my mind. In the magazine is a picture of a "small Home Roaster from £600", or "La Marzocco Linea Mini for £2,994". And that's just the mini; I was thinking of getting a proper one. So it will have to be just a book. If you are feeling religious, there is the Barista Bible, not priced, too holy I suppose, or *Water for Coffee*, £26.99.

But perhaps, after all, I'll just settle down with a slice of toast and marmalade and a mug of dear old Camp to bring me back to sanity before bedtime.

The Daily News

APRIL 2016

FUNERAL COSTS KEEP RISING

Eighties

WHEN YOU PASS into your eighties, you enter a different world, incomprehensible to young kiddies in their early sixties or even fifties and who are still at work. They just cannot understand that you are living on another planet.

Oh, don't worry – we'll take you out to lunch. There's just the four of us, it'll only be a couple of hours... afterwards we'll all pop over and see Peter and Jackie at...

They don't seem to realise that going up to London is quitee an effort, even though it's only about 40 miles. They seem to expect you to behave as they do, forgetting that 65 is the age for retirement. People like me are not just 10 years beyond that, we are nearly 20 years beyond it.

It's difficult for us to take in and we are living it; so, no wonder the 60-year-old infants can't grasp it.

Also, in your eighties, you realise you are very near The End. Most people die in their seventies; so, if you are one of the Stalwart Brigade in their Eighties, your time is almost up, chum. A relation of mine is 88 and was telling me recently that he is rather lonely. Simply because all his friends are dead. So, despite his being a very likeable, friendly chap, he is alone. Our chances of living into our nineties are pretty small, So as I am now 83, I've only got 7 years or so, at most.

Another thing which brings this

home is the tedious annual task of writing umpteen Christmas cards.

Worst of all are the absences: the deaths. The list gets longer every year, of course. As my card this year was a joke about death, it was a bit awkward. The card was simply a reproduction of a leaflet that came through the door: FUNERAL COSTS KEEP RISING, it said. Quite a wry joke for those of us in our eighties, but not much fun if your partner died a week or two ago. So, to be careful, I made a list of recent deaths. 24 in all, one an entire family – mother, father and son. Unbelievable, all 3 in their fifties and thirties.

I have received many awards down the years – not boasting, there are dozens available. But, in your eighties, the Lifetime Achievement Awards start piling in. Lifetime Achievement? This can only be awarded when your lifetime is over, surely? Have they noticed that you are not actually dead yet? Are they hinting, Come on, get a move on, we want this tidied up?

Maybe we should institute the WELLDUNALLDUN or the OVER&OUT Award, or the FINI Award.

But, better than any award is when you are told that your work has done some good in the world. Childline raised £55,000 in one month, selling Fungus and Snowman badges for £1 each.

Recently a mother wrote to say that my book *Gentleman Jim*, which is about a lavatory attendant who has ambitions to be a Company Director, was a great help to her son who suffers from Asperger's Syndrome.

Then today, an email from a lady whose 85-year-old father is suffering from Vascular Dementia. It is almost impossible for her to communicate with him, but they spent an afternoon watching *Ethel & Ernest* together. It seemed to bring him to life and they had a good talk.

Let's hope it lasts for a while.

Fireworks

YESTERDAY WAS A fun day. I nearly burned the house down. Made a change, anyway. For years we have had candles on the table for the evening meal. It's not meant to be romantic, it's just restful, and quite peaceful. Even now, when I live alone, I still do it.

It's only a two-branch candlestick, not exactly a chandelier. I always like to stick the new candle into the guttering remains of the old one, before it has gone out completely. The molten wax then trickles down, forming strange patterns and shapes before it gets to the base.

Also, the whole candle begins to lean in a direction you hadn't foreseen. It has a mind of its own.

Someone said it's like a work of art. Well, I said, if one is an artist, everything one touches tends to become Art... They gave me a funny look and left the room saying, "Got to phone Mum..."

After I've finished eating, I go into the sitting room next door for half an hour's rest and wine before starting the boring clear-up. Last night, after the rest, I went back into the kitchen and found that for the first time ever, I had not put the candles out. This is always done using the screw cap off a wine bottle as a snuffler. One candle was still burning normally but the other had burned to its end and had then ignited the wax base below. There was a fierce flame about three or four inches high and an inch or more across. A screw-cap snuffler would be useless, so I seized a big tablespoon and bashed the whole top down and out. Or so I thought.

All was well, so I retired to the bathroom and sat reading. Suddenly, there was a head-splitting noise. A kind of mechanical screaming, the voice of an insane robot. I had never heard anything like it and it was almost frightening. Clutching my trousers, I stumbled down the passage to the kitchen where the noise was even louder. When I opened the door the kitchen was a dense fog of smoke. You couldn't even see the opposite wall. I swiftly deduced that the noise was probably a "smoke alarm".

In the middle of the table was a full-blown fire with flames 18 inches high, and at table level, about a foot across.

Luckily there was a washing-up bowl in the sink full of water. I grabbed it and chucked half of it onto the flames. The fire gave a shudder but went on again almost unaffected, so I chucked the other half on. That did it. But, the mess! Liquid candle wax was set hard all over the table. My precious RNIB clock was burned black, half of it simply gone; the telescopic lamp was black and half-destroyed. Its flex had kept its shape but when touched it was semi-liquid. Sticky, black muck covered my hands and everything else.

The moral of this tale for me is: Do Not Take Risks with Anything which Relies for Safety on Your Memory. Forget something simple but vital and you could end up dead.

P.S. The following day someone pointed out a red thing which has been hanging on the kitchen door for years. I'd always meant to look at it sometime, but never got round to it. A "fire blanket" it's called. Could be quite handy, I suppose, in the unlikely event of something catching fire.

The joy of driving

ONE OF THE joys of Old Age is going out for a spin in your own motor car. So here is a Guide to Joy.

1. Approach the vehicle from the driver's side: i.e. the right-hand side when facing forwards from the rear.

2. Have you remembered to bring your Keys? If not, go back and get them. It's worth having them on a chain which is attached to a belt round your waist. You can do nothing without them.

3. Unlock the door. Don't drop the keys! You will need the Ignition Key to start the Engine. Open the door carefully. Some cars, like the Honda Jazz, have a very wide door and, if you are gazing thoughtfully into the interior whilst pulling the door towards you, you can hit yourself in the face with it.

4. Pull out the Seat Belt and let it hang down beside the back of the seat. This will make it easier to get hold of when you are seated inside. Alternatively, you can buy a short strap which attaches to the Seat Belt and enables you to pull it across yourself, without the awkward twisting round to get it.

5. Sit on the seat and swivel yourself round to face the front, at the same time negotiating your knees under the Dashboard. This can be quite awkward,

depending on the state of your knees.

6. If wearing a jacket, make sure you are not sitting on the bottom left-hand side of it. If you are, this will severely restrict the movement of your left arm when trying to manipulate the Gear Lever. Most essential.

7. Pull the Seat Belt across yourself and try to insert its metal end into the Seat Belt Socket on your left. This, too, can be surprisingly awkward, but it gets easier with constant practice. But remember! If you are in the habit of wearing your glasses on a cord round your neck, do not tighten the belt over the glasses! They will be crushed to bits.

8. Now, do not insert the Key into the Ignition Keyhole while the door is open! The car will scream a warning at you, meaning: KEY IN IGNITION! DOOR OPEN! CAR VULNERABLE TO THEFT!

9. So, reach out, if you can stretch that far and, with fingertips, attempt to slam the door shut... Uh... no good, right-hand side of jacket shut in door. Start again. Perhaps best not to wear a jacket when attempting to drive your motor car?

10. Check that the Gear Lever is in Neutral before switching the Ignition to ON. As a further precautionary measure, press the Clutch Pedal down. This will disconnect the Engine from the wheels.

11. If the Key is chained to your belt, make sure the chain is long enough to get the Key to the Ignition Keyhole; otherwise you will have to take the Key off the chain, whereupon it will, of course, fall on the floor.

12. Switch the Ignition to ON. When the Engine is running nicely, gently press the Accelerator Pedal and "rev" the engine.

13. All is set! At last! The great moment has arrived. Let driving commence.

14. So move the Gear Lever forward into Slot One (unless you want to reverse, of course). Gently let the Clutch Pedal rise, until the car moves! You are now In Gear and on your way... Hooray! At last! Joy! But no, got to get out, need a pee.

15. Always check the state of bladder before going out for a spin in your motor car.

Late in life

YES, I SAID, beaming smugly round the table, I was very lucky. I didn't need glasses till quite late in life. I was 57 at the time.

FIFTY-SEVEN, LATE IN LIFE? Ye Gods! If 57 is late in life, where am I now at 82?

Then, much earlier, working in the theatre in Bristol, one of the so-called ASMs, a school-leaver girlie of 18, said: "Yes... it must be strange for you having so much success so late in life." I was a bit put out by this as I was scarcely 40 at the time and thought I'd only just begun to get going. Of course, for an 18-year-old, anyone over 30 is on the way out. Over 40? Well, dead and gone.

Even earlier, in a café with two art teacher colleagues, one said with a groan: "Ooh... I wouldn't like to face what Harvey had last week." "Oh?" said the other, "what was that?" There was a pregnant pause, and we both feared the worst – death of a parent? Bad news from the doctor?"

"He was THIRTY!" "Oh, no!" groaned the other. Harvey THIRTY! They both fell silent and stared down into their empty coffee cups, sunk deep in gloom, trying to come to terms with the dreadful news. I kept very quiet. I was a year older than Harvey. Thirty-ONE! Suppose they found out? Would they ever have coffee with me again, or would I become an Untouchable?

I like to think that I've never

lied about my age, but I do remember once sitting outside a country pub with the wife of an old friend. I don't usually make a habit of going out drinking with other men's wives, but this was a special occasion and it was her idea.

It was 1973 and my wife, Jean, had recently died. This lady was showing me sympathy and concern, not lusting after my muscular young body. In the middle of our pleasant chat in the sunshine, she said: "How old are you?"

In a couple of months' time it would be 1974. Born 1934, and in January, which brought it even nearer. I just didn't want to say it. On top of recent events: Mum and Dad both dying in 1971, now Jean in 1973, my becoming 40 was trivial, of course, but it was the final straw.

"Oh," I said, "38, coming up for 39 soon." Pathetic. But I just couldn't bring myself to say it out loud. It's worse for women, of course, but then most things are, aren't they?

Still later in life comes the Big Switch Over. People, provided they are lucky enough to be fit and well, start being proud of their age. Yeah, still swimming twice a week... fell walking... Morris dancing... golf... charity walks... couple of marathons... they say. At what age does this start? Sixties is too early, got to be past 70 at least, but to be proud of this stuff – over 80, I would think.

So, back to the beginning: obviously, at 82 I am Late in Life, but I'm certainly not proud of it, just grateful to be so lucky. No marathons for me, but then there never were, but I can still write bits for *The Oldie*. Now, at 82, that is a great privilege. CREEP CREEP.

Oo-Oo

GETTING SENTIMENTAL? Is it wrong, unhealthy, to have a great fondness for certain objects from your own early life? I'm sure the psychs will say it is.

Have you still got your first teddy bear? I have, but I'm not all that fond of him. He was always too big and heavy for me. They say he was bigger than me when I was first given him, so that may explain it. I much preferred Oo-Oo, which was how I pronounced Wilfred, so that became his name for the following 80 years. He was Wilfred of Pip, *Squeak and Wilfred*, a long-running cartoon in the *Daily Mirror*. Pip was a big, friendly dog, Squeak was a penguin and Wilfred was a long-eared bunny rabbit, who still

sits near the end of my bed today. His worn and patchy yellow fur, his huge, floppy velvet ears now faded to a dull pink. His press button shows through the scruffy fur on his chest, but it no longer works. I can't even remember what noise it made. Poor old Oo-Oo hasn't spoken for 60 or 70 years now. His original glass eyes are long gone, too. I don't even remember what he looked like with them. My mother must have replaced them with these flat buttons, now a faded crimson and even one of these is missing. So dear old Oo-Oo is still almost blind. He has no voice, and when I prop him up on the corner of the desk to write this, he falls over backwards. Is he spineless as well? His nose and mouth, too, are almost gone. The nose was just a red V of wool with a red line leading down to another inverted woollen V for the mouth. Sadly this leaves him almost expressionless. And I've only just noticed that the poor old chap is filthy, too. After all, he hasn't washed for 80 years. You can't wash a soft toy, can you? And he can't do it himself, so that's it. Grubby old Oo-Oo goes on. For a bit, like the rest of us.

The cartoon was drawn by A B Payne, and in 1947 when I was 13 years old and an aspiring cartoonist, I wrote to him. I can't remember what I said, but was probably asking for a quick sketch. With great kindness, instead of a sketch, he sent me a fully finished drawing of Pip, Squeak and Wilfred. Pip and Squeak are excitedly watching Wilfred sign his name WILF in a big book with a long quill pen, while a tiny penguin holds the bottle of ink for him. It is signed A B Payne 3/1/47, and is one of my most treasured possessions and has been in a frame on my wall for the past 69 years.

Possibly even more treasured is my breadboard and bread knife. The knife still cuts perfectly but the lettering and design on the board have almost worn away. Still, mustn't grumble, they are almost 100 years old, just a little older than me. Once, I was even tempted to write a verse about them:

GETTING SENTIMENTAL
The breadboard I use today, and the knife,
have been with me all my life.

Mum and Dad were using them before the War.
They all survived the doodlebugs and Blitz.

After all, it takes a lot to blow a breadboard and a knife to bits.

And it takes a lot from life, to not get sentimental about a breadboard and a knife.

GET ON!
GET ON!
AAAGH!

Socks etcetera

WHEN YOU ARE OLD everything takes so long, doesn't it? Even something as simple as getting dressed in the morning takes ages. Compared with the Golden Years of Yoof, anyway; I haven't timed it yet, it seems so daft, but I'm going to do it one day soon, when there is time.

Stage One: Put On Socks. First, can I find them? Took them off last night just here at the end of the bed – only one visible now. Never mind, it's bound to turn up before long. Put the one and only sock on – aagh! Won't go on, caught on corner of sharp toenail! Take sock off, look for nail file... where is it? Used it only the other day... Uncomfortable bending knees nowadays, can

cause spasm of cramp in thighs. Consequently, tend to cut short the time spent filing toenails. At last, find nail file, half-hidden under bed, file sharp corner of little toe. Draw sock on, nice and smoothly. Well done. Well, one anyway. Halfway house.

Stage Two: Put Pants On. Not too difficult when avoiding knee-bending by sitting on corner of bed and leaning forwards. Next, Long Sleeve Thermal Vest, "The Old are always Cold". Who said that? Me probably. Important: check which is front and back, it's often difficult to tell with these things. Get it on back to front and of course, you've got to take it off and start again. Sometimes there is a badge on it which helps, as long as you can remember whether it is on the front or the back. Incredibly, some have the badge on the back.

Stage Three: The Shirt. Buttons, buttons, buttons... all up the front the button holes are vertical, but the last one, at the neck is horizontal. Why? Needs a different technique for the stiffening, aged fingers. Then, the buttons on the cuff seem to be always as far away as possible, not just on the inside where they should be, surely?

Stage Four: The Trousers. The biggest job of all. First, a leather belt which takes a slip-on leather loop with a brass hook for the Key Chain. KEYS! Vital for sanity. No Keys = no Car, no House – The End. Make sure the belt passes easily through all the trouser loops. Don't even mention Braces! That way lunacy lies. Mobile phone and handkerchief in right-hand trouser pocket, wallet, reassuringly heavy, in left-hand pocket, nearest the heart. Got to the checkout at Waitrose recently – No wallet! No cards! No cash! Had put on clean

trousers that morning and forgot to transfer the wallet. So, hand in my trolley load to the management and dash off to the bank. Luckily had cheque book (such old-fashioned useless things, aren't they?) in my bag and got cash. Saved by the Bag!

Finally, gave up searching for the missing sock. Got a clean pair from the sock drawer. Drew them both on perfectly, at last. Success! But No! Remembered the Annoying Toe Spacer. Doc says I have a burgeoning bunion, another of the joys of old age.

This is where the joint at the base of the big toe swells up and pushes it towards the others. You have to insert this rubbery wedge between the toes. And of course, in the midst of all this fiddle-de-dee, I'd forgotten it, as I almost always do. Damn, damn, damn... Off comes the sock yet again. "If at first you don't succeed..." Still, not to worry. At this age, it will not be long before you are putting your socks on for the very last time.

Someone else will take them off for you.

The magic of old ads

GOOD TASTE! WHAT a title for a magazine! And 1949! Was I alive then? It seems like a relic from another age, and yet it is only 66 years ago. What's 66 years in a lifetime? (Well, most of it, of course.)

As usual with old magazines, it is the advertisements that tell you most about life in those ancient days. First there are the dear old familiar names: Ovaltine, Marmite, Bourneville Cocoa and Jacobs Cream Crackers: "May I recommend you dear Madam to say Any Jacobs Cream Crackers in stock today?"

And AERO, but it's not chocolate here, it's special little knobs on the end of knitting needles! CHIVERS: there is a tall, elegant lady

in a long New Look coat saying: "THANKS! I'M GLAD I WAITED TILL I COULD GET CHIVERS." And there is a whole small ad just for marmalade. "CHUNKY marmalade with its delicious flavour and pre-war quality." But, oddest of all is a large picture of a vinegar bottle with the proclamation: "BOTTLED VINEGAR IS BEST." Well, what on earth else is there? Vinegar in jam jars? Barrels? Buckets? And there is OXO, of course. "OXO WORKS WONDERS, JUST ADD WATER FOR A TASTY BEEFY DRINK." Well, thank you, I'll think about it...

Then there are the usual endless ads for Inner Cleanliness: Andrews Liver Salts, Syrup of Figs, "MILK OF MAGNESIA: Golden slumbers – baby sleeps deeply and peacefully because his tummy's peaceful too. Thanks to Milk of Magnesia and a sensible Mummy."

Endless ads for hair-dos. "AMAMI Wave set – the set you desire – lovely and lasting. Both Amami's GREEN Wave Set and Amami's SPIRITUOUS Wave Set." Crumbs! GREEN HAIR? Early days of Pre-Punk? SPIRITUOUS? Must be quite uplifting and it's only 1/1 $^1/_2$ d (one and three ha'pence, yoof).

Then there are things called CAMI-KNICKERS. They look dreadful. In all my sizzling sex life I don't think I ever encountered these obstacles to progress and freedom of expression. They seem to be pants with braces attached, which would make life and lust difficult and tiresome. They would certainly put paid to that old joke about American servicemen here during the war, "One yank and they're down"' With these things you'd need half a dozen Yanks. Preferably Marines. Today cami-knickers sound more like a surveillance device – CCTV camera concealed in knickers. Take note MI5 and MI6.

Do you feel "ALIVE, CHEERFUL AND FIT" Well, no... Alive certainly, just about. Not dead... yet.

Apparently I need BILE BEANS, not to be confused with baked beans. But they don't sound very appetising... bile beans on toast?

There are endless ads for deodorants. I've never used one in my life. No doubt I should have done. Too late now at 81? Perhaps I should ask down the village shop: do I smell, Bob? Give us a sniff. Perhaps they could sell me some SNO-MIST deodorising powder. "The nicest way to ensure day long personal fresh- ness is to use SNO-MIST in the clever Puffer-pack." Sounds like something from Puffin Books.

And there is MUM, "such a simple way to guard against un-derarm odour..." And also ODO-RO-NO cream. "Stops underarm perspiration instantly."

But finally, it's back to that eternal female obsession – hair. (On head, not, this time, underarm.) Even I as a rugged elderly male must take care of my head of ash-blond hair, thus: "At the pressure of your finger tip the Kemt Mistifier radiates a sparkling spray as fine as frosted breath. As it floats upon your hair new lights of loveliness begin to glow under its magic touch." Golly, I can't wait!

OH, FLIP
THESE FLIPPING
FLEAS!

The post office

IN ALL INNOCENCE, I've just been down to our village post office to post a letter. There I was confronted by an eight-page document telling me what I could and could not post. It was just like being back at school, printed in red, grey and black, with rows of red ticks (good boy) and red crosses (bad boy). I searched through it, eager to see how many marks out of 10 I might get.

Until today I had no idea that I could not put USED ENGINE OIL in the post. What am I supposed to do with it?

Then, all my HAIR DYES and COLOURANTS – Prohibited! What about us oldies who may be going slightly silver grey? (Ash blond in my case.) Are we to be denied a little colour to lighten our last few fading years? Our equally faded lady friends are also forbidden to receive any NAIL VARNISH, POLISH or GEL. Poor old things. Just imagine an elderly lady tottering about with unvarnished nails! Can't post FROZEN WATER! Could any substance be more innocent? Besides, it might be going to a desert country where your son and his little daughter are dying of thirst? What then?

Also there are all my AEROSOLS stacked in the bathroom cupboard, DEODORANTS, BODY SPRAY (used twice daily, of course), HAIR REMOVAL CREAM, MEDICINAL AEROSOLS such as FLEA SPRAYS. Yes! What about my fleas? I don't want to become infested yet again just because of Parcel Force.

No PERFUMES & AFTER-SHAVES including EAU DE PARFUM and EAU DE TOILETTE. Frog Toilet Water! No thank you.

No LIVE CREATURES, INSECTS or INVERTEBRATES including BEES, SPIDERS and some other INSECTS (including small children?). Must be First Class marked URGENT – LIVING CREATURES – SMALL CHILDREN. HANDLE WITH CARE.

Can't send any of my drugs and narcotics either: CANNABIS, COCAINE, HEROIN, LSD, OPIUM and AMYL NITRATE. Just as well, I'm nearly running out.

No POISONS, TOXIC LIQUIDS, SOLIDS and GASES including substances that are able to cause death or injury if swallowed or inhaled or by skin contact including ARSENIC, CYANIDE, FLUORINE, RAT POISON. This is all getting a bit depressing, but wait, there is more. It gets worse.

No BIOLOGICAL SUBSTANCES including URINE, FAECES AND ANIMAL REMAINS. We all get plenty of the first two, of course, can't think of anyone to post them to just now...

No HUMAN REMAINS including ASHES. What's wrong with ashes? The deadest thing there is in the world surely? They're not going to suddenly reincarnate in a GPO sorting office, are they?

Last of all, no WASTE, DIRT, FILTH or REFUSE. Well, bit of a fag to parcel it all up. I think I'll leave it for now.

Oh, just noticed – can't send LUMINOUS DIALS FROM AIRCRAFT. Hmm... well, don't think I've got many of those.

Talking to the young lady at the counter about this leaflet, she told me they had once received a very smelly packet and thought they had better open it before sending it on. It contained a card with a large, florid female signature together with a very smelly dollop. They called the police who then went off to interview the recipient as the sender was anonymous. He did not want anything to be done, so the matter was dropped. Together with the dollop, presumably.

Eee, there's nowt so queer as folk.

Acknowledgements

Naim Attallah
for the idea.

Richard Ingrams
for his encouragement and support.

Bibliography

3. The cussedness of inanimate objects — March 2015
7. The Elephant and the Bad Baby — August 2014
9. Briggs the tea-leaf — August 2010
11. No fridge, no freezer, no flush, no fone… — September 2009
13. A chicken-and-egg situation — July 2014
16. Diving in — November 2010
18. Cycling salvation — January 2015
21. Privilege — Summer 2011
23. Touched by history — August 2011
25. Criminal brains! — January 2015
28. Digitalis — September 2011
30. Bellows humour — April 2011
33. Breaking and entering — April 2013
35. The love of a chicken — February 2015
37. Cranky, cantankerous and crotchety — November 2013
39. Money talks — March 2010
41. Telephonitis — December 2011
43. A severe blow — December 2013
45. "Got inny powst?" — October 2009
48. Bag and baggage — November 2011
50. Burning embarrassment in wartime — November 2014
52. Socialising: why make a meal out of it? — August 2009
54. The daftness of ideas about class and the idiocies of education — July 2011
56. Are crisps the new grapes? — April 2015
58. Name-dropping — February 2010
60. The ghost of Christmas past — February 2011
63. The times — April 2012
65. Bribery and lies — July 2012
67. Why bottle maid's water? — June 2010
69. The dawn of darkness — October 2012
71. Empire Day and all that — July 2013
73. Painters with plaits — September 2010
75. The appian way — September 2015
78. The naked truth — January 2011
80. Rats and registrars — July 2015
82. Three chairs! — October 2010
84. Yours ever, insincerely — June 2011
88. Shoe a Little Horse — January 2013
94. Oldie angst — February 2013
96. Great Art in Alnwick — June 2015
98. Simplify, simplify — February 2012

100. The horror of blood-red wombs — November 2012
102. The chick from the black stuff — May 2015
105. Nudes, spivs and toffs — April 2010
106. Stollidges and all that — March 2014
109. Bring back creative sociopaths — May 2013
111. All our yesterdays — April 2012
113. All tied up — Summer 2010
115. Old age adage — February 2014
117. The Excremen — October 2014
119. Let's talk rude — December 2010
121. Worlds apart — May 2010
124. The food of love? — October 2011
126. Phew! — October 2013
128. Obes, obesses and obies — May 2012
130. The back of the drawer — September 2013
132. Ireland is a very odd place — March 2011
134. Big bags and babies — March 2013
137. Has the world gone mad? — June 2013
139. England's green and potty land — September 2014
142. The joy of bodkins — June 2012
144. The Whispering Gallery &VD — July 2010
146. Who is normal? — Summer 2015
148. God's waiting room — June 2014
150. Long ago and not so far away — Summer 2014
154. My shooting times — May 2014
156. Individuality — May 2011
158. Up and on! — Summer 2013
160. Snow sadists: me and Hannibal — April 2014
162. Ladies only — December 2014
165. Art-class art and class — December 2009
167. Healthy minds, healthy bodies — September 2009
169. Apoplectic Christmas opulence — January 2012
173. Caffiends — March 2016
175. Eighties — April 2017
177. Fireworks — April 2016
179. The joy of driving — May 2017
181. Late in Life — July 2016
183. Oo-Oo — February 2017
185. Socks Etcetera — Summer 2016
187. The magic of old ads — November 2015
189. The post office — June 2016

Supporters

Unbound is a new kind of publishing house. Our books are funded directly by readers. This was a very popular idea during the late eighteenth and early nineteenth centuries. Now we have revived it for the internet age. It allows authors to write the books they really want to write and readers to support the writing they would most like to see published.

    The names listed below are of readers who have pledged their support and made this book happen. If you'd like to join them, visit: www.unbound.com.

"Ian, Suzanne, Seth and Rafe"
JK&JY
"To Gill , love Douglas 2015"
unclewilco from readersheds.co.uk
Michael Abrahams
Geoff Adams
Wyndham Albery
David Aldridge
James Allchurch
Angela Allen
Anthony Allen
Victoria Andrew
Igor Andronov
Andy Annett
Philippa Arthan
Clare Axton
Melissa Baddeley
Alan Baker
Nicola Balkind
Derren Ball
Jason Ballinger
Paul Bamford
Adrian and Annie Banham
Audrey and Edith Bannister
Sue Ann Barber

David Barlow
Bob Baughan
Juliet Bawden
Graham, Nicky and Olivia Beanlands
Adrian Belcher
Mike Bell
Heather Benson
Celia Berridge
Matt, Terri and Joseph Betts
Stephen Betts
Christine Bhatt
Ralph Birch
Peter Blackburn
Yvonne Blackburn
Claire Bodanis
Nickie Bonn
Stuart Bowdler
Richard W H Bray
Robin Bray
Paul Brazier
Greig Brierley
T. Broderick
Anne & Joe Brophy
David Browne
Lesley Bruce
Phil Bruce-Moore
Clare Bullock
Alison Burns

Chris Busby
Alex Busso
Marcus Butcher
Mike Butcher
Nigel Butcher
Jamie Byng
Peter Bywaters
John Caley
Andrew Campling
Alistair Canlin
Antonio Cantafio
Chris & Steve Carleysmith
John Carr
Micah Carr-Hill
Roger Cavanagh
Rick Challener
Jim Chancellor
Ian Christensen
Melanie Chrysostomou
Anne Clark
Thom Clutterbuck
Sam Coates
Pamela Collett
Andy Collins
Mhari Colvin
Philip Connor
Edward Cook
David Cooke
Helen Belgian Cooper
Natalie Cooper

David Cornwall
Jude Coventry
James Cox
Dawn Coxwell
Marie Craig
Luke Cresswell
Stephen Croston
Bernard (Bob) Culpin
David Cummings
Ruth Curtis
S D Ma
Geoffrey Darnton
Carol Davenport
Ian Davidson
Harriet Fear Davies
Jill Davies
Martin Leighton Davies
Alice Davis
Tony Davis
Stuart Delves
Jim Demetre
John Dexter
Guy Dickinson
Miranda Dickinson
Walter Dickinson
Maura Dpooley
Mary-Anne Driscoll
Jackie Duckworth
David Duffy
Nicholas Durbridge

Daniel Durling & Laura
  Wilson
Dave Eagle
Tony (tones) Earley
Judy Easter
Ali Edmond
Meg Edwards
Mark Ellingham
Charlotte Ellis
Richard Ellis
Simon Eltringham
Lee Essex
Bill Evetts
Terry Fahy
Pete Faint
Ronnie Fairweather
Sylvia Fairweather
Mike Fallbrown
Louise Farquharson
Sebastian R Farrell
Virginia Fassnidge
Roger Fellows
Matt Fiddes
Katy Flint
Paul Flint
Simon Ford
Alan Foster
Isobel Frankish
Sarah Frankish
Karl Franzen
Lauren Fulbright
David G Garioch
Mary Galbraith
Hilary Gallo
Mark Gamble
Griselda Garner
Alexander Lelly Gazi
Maggie Gee
Julie Gibbon
Trish Gibson
Christopher Gilbert
Joan Gilbert
Karen Gilchrist
"To Gill , love Douglas
  2015"
Marcus Gipps
Lee Goddard
Wendy Goddard
Salena Godden
Joe E Goldie
Phil Goulstone
Neil Graham
Duncan Grant
Lucille Grant
Samuel Gray

Philip Green
Paul Greer
Amy Gregson
Iwan Griffiths
Nick van der Grinten
Ruth & Hans van der
  Grinten
Valerie Grove
Vincent Guiry
Amanda Gunn
Sinéad Gunning
Jillian H Sears
Stephen Hackett
Stuart Hadley
Daniel Hahn
Janet Haines
Christine Hamill
Ann Hamblen
Miles Hanson
Paul V Harrington
Ruth Harris
Lorraine Harrison
A.F. Harrold
Caroline Harry
Elsie Hart
Caitlin Harvey
Charles Hawes
Andrew Hawkins
Vikki Hayes
Rebecca Haywood
Anthony Heath
Adin Heller
David Hemmings
Bryan Hempstead
Nathaniel Hepburn
Linda Hepper
Leigh Heseltine
Catherine Hibbitt
E O Higgins
Jez Higgins
Lisa Highton
William Hill
Bernard Hillon
Susan Hirschman
Jon Hobbs
Penny Hobson
Paul Hodges
Edward John Holloway
Federay Holmes
Mister Hope
Ann Horne
Caitriona Horne
Laura Horsley
Jo Howard
Nicholas Howard

Barrie Howe
Tiancheng Hu
Andrew Hughes
William Hughes
Alistair Humphrey
Xenia Octavia Asphodel
  Huntley
Cait Hurley
James Huxley
Penny Ives
Martin Jackson
Mark Jamieson
Patrick Janson-Smith
Hilary Jeanes
Lisa Jenkins
Kerensa Jennings
Ric Jerrom
Chris Johnson
Hayden Jones
Thomas Joy
Judith Kahn
Alex Kaula
Linda Kaye
Andrew Kelly
Christina Kennedy
Ros Kennedy
Lorna Kent
Lucy Key
Dan Kieran
George Kinghorn
Doreen Knight
Gillian Knight
Andy Knott
Teddy Kristiansen
Evelyn Laing
Ray Lakeman
Christopher Laudan
Wendy Law
Graeme Lawson
Stephanie and Jeffery Lay
Alison Layland
Ben Le Foe
Sing Yun Lee
Ben Lerwill
Caroline Lien
martin lightfoot
Judith Lindley
Daniel Lloyd
George Lloyd
Carol Long
Andre Louis
Anita Loveland
Isaac Lowe
David Luckhurst
Karl Ludvigsen

Neil Macehiter
Linda Mackinnon
Alice Magnay
Chris Maloney
Philippa Jill Manasseh
Debra Mandel
Jean Maples
Ellen Marsh
Sophie Masson
Philip Matthew
Brian Matthews
Roger Matthews
Angela Mayes
Ruth McAvinia
Tom McDermott
Chris McEwan & Carol
  Lawson
Beatrix McIntyre
Felicity Meredith
Ute Methner
Andrew Milloy
Melissa Minty
John Mitchinson
Ronald Mitchinson
Simon Monk
Ann Montgomery
Kris Moore
Matt Morden
Charles Morgan
Richard Morgan
Nancy Morris
Toby Mosbacher
Tessa Mukhida
Caroline Mullan
Jenni Murphy
Tricia Murphy - author
  of Áine
Margaux Murray
Martyn Murray
Matt Murrell
Craig Naples
Carlo Navato
New Hedgehog Bookshop
Matthew Nichols
Naomi Nile
Tess Nowell
Paul Oakley
Rodney O'Connor
G Oommen
Kaylene ONeill
A. Ottey
Gary Overall
Charlotte Owen
Jack Page
Sunil Patel

Sarah Patmore
Lucy Paul
Olivia Payne
Viggo Pedersen
Joanna Penn
Anna Perkins
Mark Persad
Gary Phillips
Catherine Pickersgill
Oliver Pickles
Adrian Pike
Tim Pilcher
Nic Piper
Frank Pitt
Lynne Pointer
Andy Polaine
David Pollard
Justin Pollard
Jean Power
Sarah Poynting
David Prew
Maria Price
Donald Proud
Jennie Pyatt
Taff Ramsey
Mark Randall
JP Rangaswami
David Rankin
Lauren Rashbrook
David Rayner
Fiona Razvi
Colette Reap
Barbara Evans Rees
Matthew Rees
Wynn Rees
Michael Rhode
Philippa Richards

Sioned-Mair Richards
Paul Rigby
Gwen Riley
Mari Roberts
Ray Rose
David Rosenthal
Catherine Rowlands
Piers Russell-Cobb
Burlap Sacking
Paul Salt
Christoph Sander
Susan Sandon
George and Patricia
    Schomburg - for all
    the kids
Helen Schultheiss
Kate & Adam Scott
Dick Selwood
John Sheehan
Hannah Sheppard
David Shriver
Melinda Skwarok
Keith Sleight
Drew Smith
Nigel Smith
Andrew 'Smudger' Smith
Barry Smyth
Philip Spedding
Antoni Spencer
Martin Spencer-Whitton
Janice Staines
Annie Stanford
Paula and Roy Stanton
Robert E. Stephenson
Annie Stevens
Cassia Stevens
Craig Stobo

Ulrike Stock
Peter Stone
Katie Stowell
David Suff
Phil Summerfield
Kevin Sumner
Dan Sumption
John Surace
Mamta Suresh
Lindsay Swann
Jess Swingler
Laura Sykes
Nick Tankard
Chris Taplin
Curtis Tappenden
Paul Taylor
Richard Thomas
Benjamin George James
    Leaver Thompson
Mike Scott Thomson
Sandy Thomson
Susan Thomson
Jeremy Timms
Annie Tomkins
Holly Tonks
Espen Torseth
Christopher Trent
Linda Tucker
Eleanor Updale
Paula Urwin
Nikki Vane
Mark Vent
Thomas Vincent-Townend
Gail Volans
Alistair Wallace
Nick Walpole
Hui-chang Wang

Nicola Warwick-Ball
Richard Wassell
Stan C Waterman
Mark Watkins
Chris Watson
Frauke Watson
Michael Watson
Orlando Weeks
Rob Welch
Kit Wells
Luke Weston
Peter Whalen
Donald Whitaker
Lena Whitaker
Crispin White
Helen White & Chris Vine
Miranda Whiting
Jason Wickham
Suzie Wilde
David Wilkinson
Evan Williams
Julia Williams
Mike Williams & Munson
    the Alaskan Malamute
Russell Willis
Damaris Wilson
Iain Wilson
Aaron Witcher
Dawn Woodger
Steve Woodward
Hannah Worrall
Michelle Worrall
Jay Wren
Alan Wright
Amanda Yam
Peter Young
Harriet Yudkin